OUT OF THE SKY

HEROISM AND REBIRTH IN NAZI EUROPE

Matti Friedman

Spiegel and Grau

S&G

Spiegel & Grau, New York
www.spiegelandgrau.com
Copyright © 2026 by Matti Friedman

All rights reserved. No portion of this book may be reproduced, stored in a retrieval system, or transmitted in any form or by any means—electronic, mechanical, photocopy, recording, scanning, or other—except for brief quotations in critical reviews or articles, without the prior written permission of the publisher.

Interior design by Meighan Cavanaugh
Map on page 7 by Andrew Roberts

Library of Congress Cataloging-in-Publication Data
Available Upon Request

ISBN 978-1-954118-98-0 (hardcover)
ISBN 978-1-954118-99-7 (eBook)

First Edition

10 9 8 7 6 5 4 3 2 1

CONTENTS

Foreword 1

1.
The Scythe 9

2.
Hannah 27

3.
Budapest 57

4.
Headquarters 65

5.
Enzo 75

6.
Haviva 95

7.
The Missing *145*

8.
Prison *163*

9.
Haim *197*

10.
Afterlife *209*

Notes on Sources 225
Acknowledgments 247
Photo Credits 249
About the Author 251

FOREWORD

Before I knew anything about the parachutists of 1944, before I read a single coded telegram, I knew them simply from their mysterious imprint on the landscape of the country where I live.

A green road sign on a highway an hour from my home in Jerusalem, for example, displays what seems like a snippet of odd poetry: the Stem of Sereni. This is a community named for Enzo Sereni, born in Rome, one of the heroes of this story. On a different road farther north, a sign directs drivers to the Flames of Haviva. The woman who gave her name to this kibbutz was a radio operator with the British intelligence outfit MI9, though Haviva wasn't the name she used behind enemy lines or the one she was born with.

And above all there's Hannah, who has not only a kibbutz named for her but also a forest and thirty-two streets. In Israel, this young woman is as famous as the ancient warrior Judah Maccabee. A few lines of verse she wrote in 1942, when she was twenty-one, are plausibly more familiar today than the words of the psalmists. More than one friend of mine remains traumatized by a school screening of the 1988 Hollywood film *Hanna's War*, starring the gorgeous Maruschka Detmers in the title role and Donald Pleasence OBE as her sadistic interrogator. Not long ago, one of my children came home with a deck of patriotic Israeli playing cards, four of which presented a select pantheon of the nation's greatest: Theodor Herzl, the founder of modern Zionism; Golda Meir, the only woman to become prime minister; the one-eyed general Moshe Dayan; and Hannah Senesh. An Israeli company manufactures Hannah figurines in a military skirt and tunic—one of these stands, saluting, on a shelf by my desk.

Anyone in Israel becomes aware that these heroes feature in some mythology situated close to the heart of this place, just as a visitor to Manhattan grasps something about America by walking down Lafayette Street, or visiting Washington Square Park. Understanding this country—an effort that has preoccupied me since I came here, like most of the parachutists themselves, as a teenager—requires figuring out who these people were and why they mattered so much. Yet beyond the barest outline of the myth, it turns out that few know anything about them. And upon further investigation, the story of these Israeli heroes turns out to be more puzzling than it first appears.

They didn't know, for example, that they were Israeli heroes. The mission unfolded four years before a country called Israel came into existence. In 1944 the land was ruled by the British. The parachutists officially served British special operations, but they weren't British either. They had no love for the British Empire but hated it less than they did the German enemy.

FOREWORD

The legend is that Hannah and the others set out at the darkest hour of World War II to save Jews and fight Nazis. But they succeeded at neither. "Who dares wins" goes the motto of one covert arm of the British military. These people dared and lost. Their actions changed nothing and yet somehow touched the fate of millions, including me. The strange gap between the mythic stature of the heroes and their scant accomplishments—this is the mystery that drew me to their story and kept me submerged in their world for years.

I wanted to ask them a few questions. Was the operation a great adventure, one of the century's most memorable feats of valor? An act of desperation, even madness? An elaborate suicide? But even the parachutists who survived to the end of 1944 are dead now. There was no one left to interview.

I did find written records, however, far more than I expected, crackling with life in the yellowing files. These yielded the story that appears in these pages. Most of the relevant documents are in an archive situated in a mansion in Tel Aviv that was once the home of a Jewish militia commander. For me, this archive was a portal to a world before the creation of the state of Israel. The authors of the documents dreamed of a Jewish state but didn't know if they'd live to see one. All around them was decimation and disaster. Every few hours I'd emerge from the archive's air-conditioning into the blinding, sweating, honking reality of this state. After hours spent photographing files in frigid air, imagining Hannah in her woolen uniform, helmet, and bulky jumpsuit, I'd come out to the boulevard to thaw on a bench, pineapple ice cream melting down my wrist, the girls of modern Israel passing in their tank tops and tattoos.

FOREWORD

. . .

IT'S IN EARLY 1944, according to the records, that army trucks take the volunteers in small groups from Tel Aviv, the new Hebrew city built on sand in British Palestine, across the Sinai desert. Their first stop will be Cairo, also under British control, where MI9 has an office in a building whose sign doesn't read "escape and evasion," obviously, but advertises a dance school. From here they'll be flown to a liberated airfield in Italy and then dropped into occupied Europe. The road through Sinai is dramatic and desolate, and in descriptions from the parachutists this journey seems like a passage between dimensions—from one life to another, or out of life altogether. In the annals of the operation, Sinai plays the same role it does in the Bible, that of an expanse to be traversed to get somewhere else. But in the story of the Exodus from Egypt, this road leads from slavery and death to freedom in the promised land. The characters in this book make the astonishing choice to travel the other way.

The operation begins as the tide of the war turns. Germany's Third Reich is starting to crumble but isn't yet close to defeat. In Russia, the Red Army has broken the siege of Leningrad after more than one million deaths and is beginning the long advance toward Berlin. In Great Britain the logistics of the D-Day invasion are secretly underway and will be unleashed in the summer. At the beachhead of Anzio, in Italy, the Germans throw the Americans back. Most of Europe's Jews have already been murdered, buried in mass graves or incinerated. In many parts of the continent the worst is past.

FOREWORD

This is not true, however, of the corner of central Europe that is the parachutists' place of origin and their final destination, the part of the continent where in 1944 the scent of the Hapsburg dynasty still lingers—a scent, I imagine, of apples, coffee, and muskets. Their Austro-Hungarian Empire expired in the previous world war and has been gone for a quarter century, replaced by rulers far worse. Budapest, the city at the center of the operation, is no longer the second imperial capital but merely the capital of Hungary, a country that is now a Nazi ally and has yet to pay the terrible price of that choice. In early 1944, as our characters begin to move into position, the boulevards are still intact, and so are the bridges linking the city's two sides, Buda and Pest, across the Danube. "I shall acquaint you with a city where, in my opinion, the beings that really matter are the houses," Antal Szerb writes of his city before the war, in *A Martian's Guide to Budapest*. "Or rather, not the houses but the erotic way they beckon to each other." The writer is still alive at the beginning of 1944, but like many others, he won't be in a year.

THIS IS A TRUE STORY. I've invented no characters, scenes, or dialogue, and have done my best to convey the events as they appear in my sources; these, should a reader wish to investigate further, are listed at the end.

"A true story." I would like to leave it there. But the uncommon intelligence and self-awareness of these characters, the way I feel them peering critically over my shoulder right now—it all makes these three words suddenly seem glib. I'm afraid this claim wouldn't

FOREWORD

pass their judgment. It's more honest to write: This is a true account of my journey into their story.

In existing accounts of the parachutists' mission there has always been confusion about who, exactly, took these young Jews who escaped the Holocaust and dropped them back in. Was it the officers of British special operations, in this case the obscure unit known as A-Force of MI9 under Tony Simonds? Or was it the determined amateurs running the proto-Mossad, the embryonic spy service of a state that did not yet exist? The cold opinion of history would have to be that it was both. But another true answer, in these pages, would be—neither. In this book, the parachutists are being dispatched by me.

These people didn't ask to become mere characters in a book written by someone they never met. Who am I to rescue them from myth and amnesia only to fit their story to my selfish specifications? What can I say in my own defense as I fold their parachute, strap them into my own literary harness, and prepare to push them out of the hatch?

Only that they were literary creatures themselves. They were authors of poems, love letters licit and illicit, at least one play, turgid ideological essays, an excellent memoir, a history of Italian fascism, and one perfect song. The heroes of this story are remembered as secret agents and commandos, but they weren't, not really. If they showed up at a military recruiting office now, they'd probably be turned away. Their talents lay elsewhere. What I mean is that I think they'd understand what I'm trying to do.

1

THE SCYTHE

In photographs from 1944 Haim appears elfin, not like a warrior at all, even in uniform. This was a particular look that Tony Simonds noticed when recruiting for MI9, and about which the British commander had a theory: "The weedy looking, delicate, shy type of people are those who are the bravest in war. Not the big six-foot-gorilla type the girls admire."

When Haim climbs the ladder into the Royal Air Force bomber at Bari, on the Adriatic coast of Italy, he's twenty-five. He sits on the hard bench with the bulk of his parachute on his back, his body vibrating with the roar of the engines. He remembers Chivvie, the British officer who escorted him to the field, "charming and slight, and yet with qualities somehow definite and masculine." When she sat next to him in the jeep with her leg pressed against his, he felt her heat through his jumpsuit.

His secret documents are in an asbestos pouch strapped to his left calf. The pouch has a fuse that can be pulled to ignite a cylinder of gunpowder that will, if necessary, incinerate the contents: a letter of introduction from MI9, a key to the radio code, and forged documents identifying him as someone other than Haim Hermesh. He considers this his real name, even if he chose it himself, the Hebrew last name meaning "scythe." At birth he was called Mihály Kaszás, while his British commanders have named him Lt. Harry Morris. His orders are the same ones given to the other parachutists who volunteered for the operation back in Palestine: Coordinate the rescue of downed Allied airmen and escaped prisoners of war behind enemy lines and establish radio contact between resistance forces and British commanders.

In a pocket he has a thin saw, the kind that can cut through prison bars, concealed in a strip of rubber. On his silk scarf is a printed map of Yugoslavia—a country that in 1944 is occupied by the Nazis and their allies, and that in our own times no longer exists. Tonight's drop zone is now in the independent state of Slovenia. Nearby is the border with Hungary, where he's to proceed when possible. Beside him in the fuselage are canisters of rifles, bullets, and anti-tank rockets bound, as he is, for the communist partisans under the famous commander Tito.

When I traveled to Bari to see what my characters saw, it was the same time of year—early summer—and I landed and took off at the very airfield used by the infiltration flights eighty years before. So it was easier than I expected to imagine the bomber with Haim inside accelerating over bleached asphalt, then lifting over grass, then above olive trees, before clearing a row of cypresses pointing at

THE SCYTHE

the sky like bayonets. The type of aircraft isn't mentioned in either Haim's memoir or in the mission files, but other parachutists specify the Handley Page Halifax, one of the workhorses of Bomber Command, here employed to drop a different kind of weapon. The aircraft's winged shadow flits across a strip of beach and onto the flat surface of the Adriatic Sea. The landscape can't have changed much. The pilot ascends into the night sky heading northeast, out of Allied airspace.

Haim's eyes close. When he opens them and looks out the open rectangle in the hull, he sees, far below, that the dark water is marked with a few twinkling lights. Haim turns to the English officer seated on the bench next to him: "A boat?"

"Nonsense," spits the officer. "You must have been asleep when we crossed the Adriatic." In fact, they're already over the drop zone in the Yugoslav mountains. Haim jolts awake. The lights are signal fires lit by the partisans. This scene is described in Haim's memoir, *Operation Amsterdam*, whose title is one of many misleading names in our story, one chosen by someone at British special operations. The idea was presumably to confuse the enemy. This story has nothing to do with Amsterdam.

The fires have been arranged in a narrow valley to form an *L*—the signal that the partisans are ready for the drop and that the pilot should proceed. The bomber's nose sinks with a deafening shriek and Haim is gripped by nausea. Wind roars through the open door. Out go the canisters, their parachutes "flapping in the wind like the wings of great bats." The pilot pulls up and banks for another run.

The red jump light comes on—ready. The sandwich and cocoa that Haim was served at the airfield churn in his guts.

OUT OF THE SKY

In one of the canisters floating down toward the forest is a small chess set for Hannah, who is already on the ground. From the partisan camps she'd sent a message to headquarters in Bari complaining of boredom, and even though the Italian port had only recently been liberated and was battered and starving, an MI9 officer had gone to search the half-empty shops until he found the game. It doesn't sound like the kind of thing they would do for just anyone.

Haim steps to the fuselage door and grips the sides, the wind whipping furiously at his knuckles. Somewhere below him are Wehrmacht camps, mass graves and deportation trains, the Gestapo lurking with dogs and Lugers. He stares up at the stars, afraid his legs will freeze if he dares look down. This is still the era before the reserve chute.

A hero needs a narrative in which actions matter and death has meaning. Otherwise it's impossible to go through the door. The story that drives Haim seems to be the one embodied in his own name: the story of Jewish rebirth as preached by Enzo, the mission commander, and by Labor Zionist prophets like A. D. Gordon, who urged a return to the simple life of the soil. This story brought the skinny Hungarian bourgeois Kaszás to Palestine in 1940 on the leaky freighter *Libertad*, defying the British destroyers hunting Jewish refugees, then changed him into the farmer-fighter Haim the Scythe. Kaszás was a victim. The Scythe is a man of the land, an avenger. If his parents and neighbors are trapped in Europe, three full trains of them leaving for the death camps every day, he'll fly in to save them like a bat with silken wings.

The green light blinks on. The jumpmaster slaps Haim's shoulder, opening the next and possibly last chapter in his short life. The

THE SCYTHE

sandwich and cocoa somersault inside him and rise in his throat. He flings himself into the air and throws up at the same time, the vomit blowing back in his face.

THE VIOLENT UPWARD FORCE when the parachute opens, the canopy spread above his head, his legs swinging in the air—it's strange, but these calm his stomach and nerves. He wipes his cheeks and mouth and grips the shoulder straps, finding them "strong and solid."

Strong and solid. This is a person suspended between a British airplane and a continent occupied by Nazis. His old country is dead to him, and his new one not yet born. Many of his childhood friends have vanished into a system of industrial murder. He detests the British for turning back desperate refugees fleeing the Nazis in order to placate Arab sentiment, for reneging on their promise of a Jewish home at the moment when it was most needed, for boarding the *Libertad* when it approached Palestine and jailing him in an internment camp when he was only running for his life. It's not much remembered now that the first shots the British fired in anger in World War II, on September 2, 1939, seem to have been aimed not at Germans but at the refugee vessel *Tiger Hill*, killing two Jews trying to reach safety. Haim swore an oath to their king and is wearing their hated uniform because it's his only way to get behind enemy lines, given that the Jews have no air force.

When Haim wisely checked the first parachute he was issued at the airfield in Bari, he found that it was worm-eaten and useless. When he complained, the British quartermaster simply blamed the damp and the carelessness of the Italian warehouse workers and issued him a new one without apology. The first two members of the group who'd been sent into Europe, jumping into Nazi-allied Romania, were dropped by the Royal Air Force forty miles off target and landed not just in a hostile town but next to a police station. After being arrested and then released in a prisoner exchange, one of the pair warned his comrades to beware the English: "They're as dangerous as the Nazis."

Any soldier knows that carelessness is one of the dangers of military service, and I learned this myself in Israeli uniform. But it's hard not to suspect that agents like Haim are expendable. The British are happy to use foreign volunteers for operations in Europe. They need people who speak local languages and know the territory—histories of the Special Operations Executive are full of these colorful and forlorn figures. Most, as I learn from the historian Eric Morris, "were not around long enough to leave a record of their existence and they vanished without a trace."

THE HOWL OF THE BOMBER ENGINES wanes to a whine and then a hum. The sky goes quiet. Now Haim lies on his back on wet grass. He looks up at the stars and breathes a scent he recognizes from his past—soil, cow dung, cooking fires. It has been four years since he fled, trading these European smells for Levantine ones like scorched pine trees and anise. A shadow bends over him with a rifle and bandolier.

Haim starts as the shadow extends a hand and introduces itself as Sgt. Grandeville of British intelligence—but his English is spoken

THE SCYTHE

with a German accent. The sergeant quickly explains that he was born in Austria, and doesn't need to explain that Grandeville isn't his real name. Most of the people here aren't who they say they are. The British officer in charge, for example, a Major McAdam, is not a Scot but a Frenchman, an officer loyal to de Gaulle who defected from the Vichy collaborators; Simonds of MI9 records that this "McAdam" was in fact from the French Caribbean colony of Martinique.

Across a field, Haim sees moonlight reflected off the low walls of a village. He has landed on target in northern Yugoslavia, near the Hungarian border. He gets to his feet as partisans move quickly around him—they've spent the night waiting for the airdrop and are worried about German spotters and spies. They need to reach cover before dawn. The fighters extinguish the signal fires, gather the canisters, and scatter. As Haim is hustled across the dark field to the village, he asks Sgt. Grandeville about Hannah. The sergeant knows whom he means. As a woman parachutist in British uniform, the only one in the sector, she was a novelty. But she's moved on, the sergeant says, and he doesn't know where she is now.

AFTER A FEW HOURS of sleep in a farmer's cottage, Haim wakes in daylight. An officer in British uniform is seen approaching the village on foot. When the man nears the cottage, dusty and gaunt, Haim recognizes Reuven Dafni.

Dafni is another parachutist from Palestine, a member of an agricultural collective on the Sea of Galilee, and before that a kid from these parts—a Yugoslav Jew from Croatia, one of few still alive in 1944. The fascists, Germans and locals, have been thorough. He's been here for three months, moving with the partisans, keeping to the wooded hills while German troops occupy the flatlands. As socialists, the Jewish parachutists don't believe in rank among themselves, but because Dafni knows the country and speaks the local Serbo-Croat, Haim defers to him.

The partisans have a truck that runs on logs—a photograph of this wondrous vehicle survives in the files. When it's available, Haim and Dafni can use it to transport their radio and the rest of their gear, but the truck is in demand, so Tito's men also give the two parachutists a porter, a sixteen-year-old who concealed himself in a closet while the fascists killed his parents. Their crime had been hiding their pigs to avoid confiscation. The kid has sad eyes and a bad heart, which is why he can't fight. He comes with a mule.

"THE PINE FOREST GREETED US with the darkness of the plagues of Egypt," Haim writes. "Skies covered with leaden clouds sprayed our heads with thin rain." The partisans move under cover of the trees and at night to evade the Storks, the slow Luftwaffe spotter planes that hunt them by daylight. They pass through the blackened shell of a Croat village flattened by German bombers, the sole inhabitant an old man who lingers like a shade, begging the partisans for bread. The fighters move fast even though some of them are barefoot—let them get too far ahead and you'll never find them again. They know the places to relax and the stretches where it's best to run, the secret paths through the forest, and the routes that the Nazis use by the roads and railways. The guerrillas strike from the forested hills at the Germans and collaborators farther down the slopes and in the valleys. Haim learns quickly. He greets comrades with the partisan motto, which you're supposed to pronounce with passion, fist raised: *Smrt fašizmu! Sloboda narodu!* Death to fascism! Freedom to the people!

He's popular with the fighters for bringing their first PIAT rockets, particularly after they try one out on a gendarmerie building in an occupied town. The partisans return jubilant, and one embraces him: The British lieutenant will be gratified to hear that they left German remains stuck to the wall, "like stamps in my little brother's album."

SOMETIMES THE AIRPLANES over the partisan camps are German. Sometimes, flying higher and in greater numbers, they're the Allied bomber fleets passing through to bomb the oil fields at Ploiești, in Romania, which fuel the Nazi armies. The bombers face enemy fighter planes and antiaircraft guns, which is why MI9 needs people on the ground below the flight path. In Cairo, Tony Simonds runs the escape lines across the Mediterranean and up into the Balkans. The parachutists help round up the ragged Britons, Americans, Canadians, or New Zealanders who drop periodically into the forest. They radio headquarters to arrange extraction on little planes that hit the secret partisan runways and take off again for Allied airfields, where these lucky men can be fed back into the war.

Haim is moving among the trees one day when he sees trunks that are burned and broken. A few steps later he finds half of a

British bomber jutting into the air. Next to it is a white parachute, a good sign. There might be a survivor nearby.

But when he draws closer, he sees that the silk is blackened and torn. What remains of the airman is strewn on the ground nearby. There's a fragment of skull, some brain. Whoever this was jumped too late. A few partisans are near the wreck with kids from a nearby village who must have seen the plane go down. One of the kids hands Haim a photo he took from the pilot's body, a color shot of a woman in uniform, inscribed, "All my love to you—Dixie."

He records the engine's serial number so he can radio it to MI9. That's his mission. Or so the British believe.

THE FILES OF THIS OPERATION can be found in the Tel Aviv mansion that once belonged to the militia commander Eliyahu Golomb. The mansion also served as a secret headquarters of the Hagana, whose name is Hebrew for "defense." This is the Jewish underground army at the time of our story, when the British still run the country, which they call Palestine, and when the Jews, who call it the Land of Israel, alternate between cooperation and rebellion. (The Arab residents tend to reject both names, and instead view themselves as part of the greater Arab nation that stretches across much of the region and is beset by colonialist invaders imposing new states and artificial borders.)

Before Haim left for Europe, he attended a clandestine meeting in Tel Aviv with Golomb and other chiefs of the Zionist movement in Palestine, soon to become leaders of the State of Israel. One of them was the future prime minister David Ben-Gurion himself—a

THE SCYTHE

measure of the importance of this operation. With a few of his comrades, Haim sat in his new British uniform. They'd come to be informed of their real mission.

The meeting was held in secrecy because the operation had to be kept not just from the Germans, but also from the British, even though the parachutists themselves were now British soldiers. None of the officials in the room was an intelligence professional, but many had come up through underground groups of Zionists or socialists in their country of origin, and thanks to an education provided by the dictators and secret police of Europe, clandestinity wasn't something they needed to be taught. To the young volunteers, the leaders are figures of great age and experience—but Ben-Gurion, known as the Old Man, is only fifty-eight. The Jews in Palestine are impossibly young, and many of them are newly orphaned.

For decades the Zionists have been trying to initiate Jews into action and strength, to shake them from passivity and awaken them to self-reliance in the Land of Israel. To this end, they've jettisoned the old Jewish role models, meek scholars and rabbis, and elevated new ones. In Zionist kindergartens the songs are about formerly minor figures like Judah Maccabee, leader of the revolt against the Seleucids in the second century BCE, or the guerrilla commander Simon Bar Kokhba, who was traditionally detested by Jewish sages for leading a disastrous uprising against the Romans in 132 CE, now reborn as a glorious fighter. The Zionists have a new ethos. But without a state or army they've still been helpless to stop the slaughter of the Jews of Europe. This maddening dissonance pervades the room in Tel Aviv.

The operation has two parallel commands: the British officers of MI9 in Cairo and the Zionist leaders in Tel Aviv, who recruited the volunteers from among European escapees. The British believe they are taking advantage of the talent and motivation of one tiny group under their rule; the Jewish commanders, on the other hand, refer to the British as their "partners," as if a group of stateless dreamers is the equal of the world's greatest empire. The British think they're using Jewish parachutists, natives of occupied countries, for their war aims; the parachutists believe it's they who are using the British, and they sometimes refer to the entire MI9 operation as nothing more than a "plane ticket." The real mission is to save Jews.

At the meeting before the parachutists' departure, this goal was clear to everyone in the room. It just wasn't clear what precisely this would mean once they landed.

The militia commander Golomb told the young recruits that their job was to reach surviving Jews and train them for combat. Everyone knew about the ghetto uprising the previous year in Warsaw, where a small group of heroes led by young Zionists held off the Nazis for weeks with breathtaking courage before they were crushed. It was intolerable that millions of other Jews seemed to be going passively to their deaths. Golomb wanted more uprisings.

Another official at the meeting gave the parachutists a contradictory directive: Their mission, he said, was to find Jewish refugees and help them stay alive until the end of the war. There was no point in military action that was certain to fail. Golda Meir, another future prime minister of Israel, was also present. She said little but teared up, understanding that these young people wouldn't all be coming back.

THE SCYTHE

Left unstated by the people in the room was the need to gain combat experience with the British so that one day soon, at the moment of truth after the world war, these skills could be used against the British themselves. In order to gain independence, the Jews would have to throw off British rule before facing the Arab world. This British operation was, in other words, also an operation against the British. An awareness of this fact on the British side explains why imperial bureaucrats regularly dampened Jewish enthusiasm about forming units to fight the Nazis, and why they'd quashed the original Zionist plan for this mission, which was to raise an entire battalion of paratroopers who'd be dropped behind enemy lines to lead a Jewish revolt. The Jews had the men and the motivation, but British officials worried that arming Jews would boomerang against Britain after the war. They weren't wrong. In the end, the total number of parachutists was just thirty-two.

When the lesser leaders were finished, Ben-Gurion finally spoke, presenting his own version of the mission. The British, he told the people he was sending to serve in British uniform, had cruelly shut the gates of the Land of Israel to refugees, condemning millions of Jews to death at Nazi hands. The Jewish pioneers in the country weren't numerous or strong enough to break open the gates on their own, so the Jewish nation must batter them from the outside. Ben-Gurion was already thinking less about the world war than about the day after it ended. The parachutists were to prepare survivors for mass immigration, priming a human tide that no one could stop. "After the victory," he said, "all the roads of Europe, all the railway tracks, and all of the rivers will bear witness to the vast flow of Jews making their way to the Land of Israel. Remember: this is your duty."

Multiple versions of the "real" mission were presented at the meeting in Tel Aviv. But the elusive nature of the events requires more time to unravel—the characters aren't deep enough in Nazi Europe, and things haven't yet gone off the rails. The real mission, in my view, is one that no one heard stated outright, then or later. But accepting these conflicting plans at face value, what they have in common is apparent: Not one is remotely in the grasp of barely thirty people sent into multiple Axis countries in twos and threes.

Haim remembered leaving the meeting confused. But he didn't drop out, and neither did anyone else.

AT ONE OF THE PARTISAN CAMPS in Yugoslavia a report reaches Haim of Jews hiding in the forest nearby. Most of those who once lived in these parts have been murdered or have fled, and this is the first he's heard of any still alive in the vicinity. With another parachutist, he sets out to find them. On a path through the trees, the two soldiers are stopped by an apparition—an old man in a ragged suit and gold-rimmed spectacles.

Smrt fašizmu! says the man. Death to fascism!

The second parachutist answers in Hebrew: *Shalom.*

The old man looks at the two soldiers. Today the sight of Jewish soldiers may not seem odd, because the revolution sought by Haim and his comrades will succeed. But here, in the early summer of 1944, this vision must hardly seem credible. The bespectacled man bursts into tears. Other figures emerge from among the trees, dozens of them, then more than a hundred—old people, women, and children. There are no young men.

THE SCYTHE

The refugees shout questions in German, Serbo-Croat, and Yiddish. Haim understands that they were interned in an Italian camp, escaped when the fascist regime of Mussolini collapsed, and have been wandering for months. He finds that he too is crying, and can't speak.

In his next transmission to headquarters, Haim asks his British commanders to fly the refugees to safety. But space on Allied aircraft is scarce and reserved for military personnel. MI9 needs trained aircrew who can be put on new bombers, not useless civilians. Haim knows this. The position of the Western Allies is that the particular problems afflicting Jews in this war will be solved by the general defeat of Nazism, which is why no airplanes are ever sent to disable the death camps. There is not a country on Earth that prioritizes saving these people to the extent that their enemies prioritize killing them.

The parachutist from the Land of Israel, Haim the Scythe, can tell the people in the forest a story: There's a place for them in the world, the same one they know from the Bible. He made it there himself, then flew back to this hell and jumped from an airplane to reach them. Maybe knowing this will give them strength to survive a while longer. Other people control the planes, the ports, and the sea. He has nothing to offer but this story.

THROUGHOUT THIS TIME, Hannah Senesh is an enigmatic presence and absence. She was here in this sector, but now she's gone. She's up the river. There are conflicting rumors. She's alive in the belly of the beast but can't transmit—or she has transmitted, it's just not clear to whom. The possibility that she has been caught or killed is too terrible to speak aloud.

Dafni, Haim's comrade, was with Hannah when she jumped on March 11. He was also among the last to see her before she crossed on foot into Hungary on June 9, carrying a British transmitter in a leather suitcase and intending to catch a train to Budapest at a rural station across the frontier. One report says she managed to board. Another even says she successfully reached Budapest, the city of her birth, and made contact with the local resistance. But the truth is that there has been no word from her at all. In the first weeks after his arrival, Haim unfurls his antenna every day at the appointed time, readies his wireless set, and waits for her transmission from across the border. Eventually he gives up. The chessboard he brought for her isn't mentioned again.

Everyone in these parts seems to have known Hannah Senesh, or at least to have heard of her. Tito's partisans include women, but the resistance fighters are fascinated, one of the parachutists records, by "the young British officer smart in her army uniform, pistol strapped to her waist." In a memoir that Tony Simonds of MI9 writes three decades later, he describes her as "brave and beautiful," and although he misremembers many other names, he gives the Hungarian spelling of hers, "Szenes," with improbable accuracy. (I'm using the spelling by which she became known to the English-speaking world after the war.) Someone looking at photographs today would not necessarily describe her as beautiful, but her contemporaries do, with a recurring emphasis on her eyes.

A Canadian major attached to the partisans, William Jones, is moved to write to a friend in Jerusalem later that same year: "I had the pleasure of meeting a young lady from Jerusalem who parachuted to my headquarters in Slovenia and then proceeded overland to another part of Europe." Hannah isn't from Jerusalem, but that's who he means. "She was a grand girl and as plucky as anyone could be. Should you hear of her when she returns, please put yourself out to meet her. She was accompanied by two other young men from Palestine. They were all excellent and will be regarded as great heroes as time goes on."

By the time the Canadian writes those lines, Hannah is nearly beyond human contact.

2

HANNAH

The first entry in her file reads, "Agrees to any job."

This agent file—a large card to which a photograph of Hannah has been glued, with text in handwritten Hebrew—is prepared by Jewish commanders choosing candidates for referral to Simonds at MI9. When she first appears for vetting, the candidate is twenty-two. Her birthplace is Budapest. She arrived in Palestine four years earlier, in the fall of 1939, just as the war broke out. At the time of her selection, she's proficient in Hebrew; fluent in Hungarian, German, and English; and passable in French. She'll be given the Hebrew code name Hagar and the British designation Mini. The chronological entries on the card unfold over precisely one year—from November 1943 to November 1944.

The first entries are written by Enzo Sereni. Enzo is a guide, teacher, psychologist, and father, someone who speaks from the reassuring height of his thirty-nine years. He's also the parachutists' direct superior in the Zionist command chain, the one that functions parallel to the British MI9 commanders. A writer from an aristocratic clan of Roman Jews, converted from Italian nationalism to Zionism by the advent of Mussolini's Fascisti, and then disabused of his pacifism by the Nazis; a fiery man who loves his wife—who has her own heroic role to play in this story—among others; a man whose drinking is occasionally noted with concern by his comrades; the author of a 1936 book about Jewish-Arab cooperation under Zionist socialism, which now reads as touching and delusional; a passionate emissary of the Zionist movement sent to awaken the Jewish youth of Germany, New York, and Baghdad to the dangers of their time and to the dream of a Jewish state. For the parachutists, the great drama of their lives often begins with a cryptic note from Enzo—a summons from their remote agricultural communes to a meeting in Tel Aviv.

Those who pass vetting are sent to parachute training at a Royal Air Force field in Galilee before being driven across the desert to Cairo for final preparations and instruction in Morse code. The recruits are speakers of useful central-European languages, newcomers, members of Zionist youth movements now milking cows or planting lettuce. They are terrified for their families in Europe, tormented by their own relative safety and by their inability to help. Haim the Scythe records his moment of decision, which followed the arrival at his kibbutz of a child refugee who turned out to have a secret letter written on a piece of fabric sewn into the lining of his coat. The Jews under Nazi rule, this letter began, were "hunted like wild animals," and the details chilled his blood. We are unfortunate, in our times, to be accustomed to ideas like death camps and gas chambers, and it's hard to remember that in those days an ordinary

HANNAH

human brain struggled to grasp that such things could exist. That night he couldn't sleep and walked out into the fields, feeling tiny under the winter stars in the distant Middle East. At dawn, still awake, he had decided that whatever the risk, he was going back.

The recruits take buses to Tel Aviv over dusty roads shaded by eucalyptus trees, or hitchhike with trucks carrying eggs to market. Enzo awaits each of them at the appointed time. In one account, the Italian stands on the rooftop of a building on Allenby Street, examining the new arrival from behind round glasses. "The dangers of the mission are clear to you," he asks, "are they not?"

The honest answer is no, but the right answer is yes.

"THE DAY AFTER TOMORROW I'm starting something new," writes Hannah to Gyuri, her older brother and only sibling. He's stranded in France, where he was studying when the war broke out. Their mother, Katherine, is trapped in the family house on Rose Hill in Budapest. From an office in the same city, the SS *Obersturmbannführer* Adolf Eichmann is about to oversee the efficient murder of the last intact Jewish community on the European mainland. Hannah's father, the playwright and novelist Béla Senesh, has been spared these events only by dying when his daughter was six.

"Perhaps it's madness," she writes. "Perhaps it's fantastic. Perhaps it's dangerous. Perhaps one in a hundred—or one in a thousand—pays with their life. Perhaps with less than their life, perhaps with more. Don't ask questions. You'll eventually know what it's about."

HANNAH

. . .

THE ENTRIES IN HANNAH'S AGENT FILE begin when she's twenty-two. They are written by other people—by the men ushering her to her fate. But we have earlier entries, and in her own voice, in the diary she started in Budapest at age thirteen. It begins, like the agent file, with a physical survey. "I'm glad I've grown lately," writes Hannah—or not Hannah, exactly, because she hasn't yet adopted a Hebrew name and is still known as Anna, or Aniko to family and friends. "I'm now five feet tall and weigh ninety-nine pounds. In my opinion, and also in the opinion of others, I'm not a pretty girl, but I'm hoping this changes for the better."

A few months later, April 1935: "We got our class reunion rings today. We'll meet on May 1, 1945. Ten years from now! What a long time! How many things can happen between now and then."

Everything in the diary takes on a different meaning later. She can't imagine how wrong she is about this future meeting, or how perceptive her sense of the number of things that can happen.

THAT SUMMER she turns fourteen.

> *I wrote only two poems all summer, one for Mama's birthday and the second—about which I was too embarrassed to tell anyone—on the subject of life, again. My fate must be to become a philosopher, because everywhere I look I see life in miniature: in a day (morning, afternoon, evening); in a river (source, flow, estuary); in a year (spring, summer, autumn, then*

the sleep that is winter). In each there is birth, life, and death. This is why I'm constantly thinking about life and death. It's not the romanticism of girls who are afraid they'll never marry and will die young, but thoughts about the eternal laws of nature.

In October she's at the cinema.

Tuesday, the 22nd, was the premiere of a film based on Daddy's play Terminal. *Paul Hörbiger is quite charming as the lead. His costar is Maria Andergast. The whole film is really delightful; I was very happy about that, as I was so nervous about it before. I don't know why. It wouldn't have been Daddy's fault if it turned out poorly, since the play itself was so good.*

Now it's 1936, and she's fifteen. She has just written a play herself and performed it for a teacher, her "first premiere."

I wrote the play and directed it, it was quite a lot of work, but I think Miss Boriska wasn't able to appreciate it. I believe the play was quite good, though nothing spectacular. In any case it didn't make a conclusive statement. As far as a profession is concerned, I'm still leaning toward studying hotel management.

She puts up with a string of disappointing boys her age, including one named Tomi.

Just to note that Gyuri was kind and sweet yesterday. One of the boys said he didn't understand what Tomi sees in me, since

> *I'm nothing special. Gyuri answered that I'm very smart, and that even though I never study, my grades are all excellent. The boy answered, "Well, that is something!" But I think that from a boy's perspective intelligence in girls is not a priority. A girl must have certain other attractions. This is very evident in the novel* Vanity Fair.

She confides her dream for the future:

> *My desire, still and always, is to be a writer—I want to be a writer. I don't know if this is a longing for glory, or a desire to be seen, but it's such a wonderful feeling when one writes something good that I believe this is worth striving for. People who are above average usually experience deeper pain, but also greater joys—and I would rather choose that than the life of an average person. I don't even mean writing as a profession. I don't necessarily think that it's famous people who are above average, but rather people with great souls. And I want to be a great soul.*

The next day, August 4, 1936, she has second thoughts. "When I reread what I wrote, I was angry with myself. Now every word looks like an artificial phrase, like a pretense. 'A great soul!' How distant I am from that. I'm a 15-year-old girl waging a petty struggle with the trifling things of life, and struggling mostly with myself."

She turns sixteen. She senses that the tenuous acceptance of people like her family, Jews who have sought a place in Budapest society without conversion or concealment, is beginning to ebb. She's back from a trip to Italy, spending the rest of her summer vacation with family and friends outside the city.

> *At first the beach seemed terribly tiny, but apart from that I enjoyed not having to sit alone with a book—though to be honest, that wasn't so bad either....*
>
> *It's already clear there won't be any real company for me here. There are Christian boys, but the segregation is so stark here that it's almost unthinkable for a Christian boy to interact with a Jewish girl. Sometimes this segregation seems almost laughable, though in truth it's rather sad and troubling.*

On New Year's Eve 1937, she's at the theater for the premiere of a new comedy.

> *The play,* Sweet Home, *was quite weak. I couldn't help thinking about the premieres of my father's plays—I think there was more applause and genuine laughter at those. And somehow I had this powerful longing for them to perform one of my plays and for the audience to cheer wildly, not rush to the cloakroom after the third act.*

After this, world events begin to penetrate her inner world in earnest. In March, before she turns seventeen, she listens on the radio as Nazi troops occupy neighboring Austria and are greeted by cheering crowds in Vienna. "The events have caused indescribable tumult for us as well. They were discussed at school, on the streets, even at parties." In a train compartment the following month, she fends off a young man, a Protestant theology student, who insists on talking to her even when she hides behind a book (*The Moon and Sixpence* by W. Somerset Maugham), and becomes angry when she won't tell him her name. It's clear, she records him saying, "that we Jews rigidly withdraw from contact and social mixing." In the same entry she notes "great tension" as parliament debates a new bill to restrict the rights of Jewish citizens. "We'll see," she writes, "how this all ends."

At her high school, she wins election as head of the literary society only to be informed that a Jew may not hold this position. By the fall she's applying herself less at school and is instead taking private lessons in Hebrew. The entry for October 27, 1938, doesn't read "I've become a novelist." It reads, "I've become a Zionist."

MY FAVORITE IMAGE of Hannah is a photograph taken around this time, when she was seventeen, in the family house in Budapest. She's wearing an elegant dress and reaching up to a high shelf to select a book. Because I've always wondered which story could have been powerful enough to push her out of the airplane, I become fixated on the idea that it's this very book. The fact that no title is visible allows my imagination free rein.

Maybe it's one of the novels or plays that made her father famous enough for some of the prison guards to recognize her last name. But most of Béla's work is in the genre of light comedy and so seems unlikely as a source of heroic stimulus. *War and Peace* is an obvious candidate—in her diary she writes that she admires Tolstoy's masterpiece, even if her interest flagged near the end. But the book she's holding is far too slim. Maybe it's Madách's play *The Tragedy of Man*, in which she once played the archangel Michael in a school production. Or a book of stories like the ones collected in *Czechoslovak Fairy Tales: 15 Czech, Slovak and Moravian Folk and Fairy Tales for Children*, the kind that introduced the sleepy children of Europe at bedtime to good and evil, to the imperative of ennobling one's life with a quest. "By late afternoon they had crossed the last mountain, had left behind them the last stretch of dark forest, and they saw looming up ahead of them the Iron Castle. Just as the sun sank the prince and his followers crossed the drawbridge and entered the courtyard gate. Instantly the drawbridge lifted and the gate clanged shut."

Or maybe the inspiration came from a different world of literature?

Hannah's diary from October 7, 1934—five years before she escaped to Palestine, nine years before she's recruited. She's thirteen. "Those afternoon services are so odd; it seems one does everything but pray. The girls talk and look down at the boys, and the boys talk and look up at the girls—this is what the entire thing consists of."

At the great synagogue on Dohány Street in Budapest women sit on a high balcony below the dizzying patterns painted on the ceiling, looking down at the men in the pews on the ground floor. The books that are read aloud here in their yearly cycle, the Torah and the prophets, convey the Jewish instinct for taking defeats and tragedies and transfiguring them through words into moral victories, or at least lessons. Even if the girls at Dohány Street did spend the prayer service talking and looking at the boys, the ideas were in the air, accessible to an intelligent young person. Assyria, Babylon, and Rome had better armies, but the Jews had better stories, and these are still read every week. Heroes like Moses, Joshua, and Deborah did what they were called to do, and live forever in these books. The enemy recurs in shifting forms—the Babylonian king Nebuchadnezzar, the Amalekites who attack from behind, the Persian vizier Haman—but the real enemy is inside us, in our own selfishness and cowardice, our heedlessness of the divine.

Another child who came to this same synagogue, and who in fact lived in the building next door to it, was Theodor Herzl. The prophet of political Zionism was born in Budapest sixty years before Hannah, and his parents registered him in the communal rolls at Dohány Street when he turned thirteen. Herzl was a playwright and a journalist, like Hannah's father, but that work hasn't lasted, and Herzl's most famous line is a political exhortation: "If you will it, it is no dream." The dream is to liberate the Jews from the malevolent fantasies of their neighbors and see them reborn as free people in their own country. Herzl sensed, better than nearly anyone else, the coming catastrophe and saw the need for a solution as radical as the threat. In 1895, gripped by a kind of ecstatic vision in a Paris hotel room, he put this idea into words in a pamphlet called *The Jewish State*. It wouldn't be enough—his own daughter, Trude, would die in a Nazi camp. The site of the building where he was born, next to the synagogue on Dohány Street, now houses a mass grave from the winter of 1944. But *The Jewish State* is one of the most influential texts ever written, proof that a story can alter reality, and Hannah certainly knew the book. This could be the one she's holding in the photograph. But I don't think so—the volume seems too thick.

OUT OF THE SKY

. . .

Six months after escaping Budapest and joining Herzl's acolytes in the Land of Israel, she's in horticulture class at the farming school for girls at Nahalal. As far as the future goes, she's thinking about milking cows. The Jews don't need more intellectuals. The Zionist pioneers worship muscle and courage and look down on people who talk too much, whose manners are too fine. She keeps her poetry to herself. She's eighteen.

I came to this country at the same age to work in a dairy barn, as it happens, and did so for a year. I wasn't running away from anything, at least not anything I could put my finger on. Maybe the unease of being part of a minority, even in a polite city like Toronto, where I grew up. Maybe it was the pale future that seemed to await me. I wasn't running for my life, like Hannah, but like her I was drawn to a new way of living, one that didn't force a Jew to live apart from society or in perpetual tension with the majority. I landed in cow shit. I still miss the sleepy teamwork of a dawn in the milking parlor, the smooth flanks of the beasts, the steam of their glistening nostrils. One of the most beautiful memories I have is from that same age, eighteen—a moment spent standing on alfalfa bales that I had just stacked four high with a front-end loader on the edge of Mount Gilboa, looking across the fields and fishponds in the valley, understanding that I wasn't going to be able to leave.

But peeling potatoes in the communal kitchen, and folding thousands of socks in the laundry, makes Hannah wonder about manual labor. She must be meant for something else. "I know that I won't be a simple worker. I can't be and don't want to be," she fumes in her journal, which she now writes in Hebrew. She has low moments when she wonders if she erred in coming here at all, and if she can ever be forgiven for abandoning her mother.

On the day of the diary entry from April 10, 1940, her horticulture instructor is teaching the class about the role of root cells. These cells, Hannah records, "are the first to penetrate the earth and prepare the way for the entire root. In the meantime, they die." Hannah may not be meant for horticulture, but she knows a metaphor when she sees one. She thinks about the young pioneers she's met since she arrived to begin her new life, people who've spent years battling drought and the soil and their neighbors, whose faces are lined beyond their years. Is the role of her generation of Jews, she wonders, the same as the role of the root cell?

"These questions," she writes, "are of far greater interest to me than the study of botany."

BEFORE HER WRITING STOPS abruptly at twenty-two, when she's muzzled by the demands of the mission and restrictions of field security, Hannah seems both mature beyond her years and not quite a grown-up, the kind of serious young person who channels their formidable vitality into ideas instead of sex. She has a few suitors, but they aren't what she's looking for. One tries to kiss her; she rejects him, then wonders why. She's not like the native-born Jews her age, the sabras, bred for a kind of heedless physicality. She's between countries and languages and phases of life. She's a chrysalis. A reader of her diary is seized with hope that she will somehow emerge, with these same powers of observation, into adulthood.

When she begins the study of poultry, including the incubation of chicks, a new agricultural metaphor presents itself. "Nothing I do makes any sense," she writes on April 12, 1941.

> *I need people, not just hunks of flesh, people close to me in thought, in feeling. Not even "people." Just one person. I fear that inside me is a hidden thermostat that keeps me from heating up or cooling off too much. This uniform temperature is good for raising chicks, for growing the embryo inside the egg. But it kills the young human.*
>
> *Why am I so lonely?*

She takes a walk after dark through the village of Nahalal, outside the farming school.

> *It was a beautiful starry night. Little lights twinkled on either side of the broad road, and in the middle. From afar I heard sounds of music, singing, conversation, laughter. I heard dogs barking as if from a great distance. The houses were far away, and only the stars were close. I was seized by a sudden fear: Where is my life leading? Will I keep walking alone at night, looking at the twinkling stars, thinking they're close to me, and not hearing the singing, talking, and laughing all around me, never turning off the road to go into the little houses? Should I choose the lights that are weak and close, beckoning me from the cracks in the walls of the homes, or the distant light of the stars? And even worse—when I'm with the stars I miss the little lights, and when I go into one of the houses my soul yearns*

HANNAH

for the heavenly bodies. Inside me there is discontent, a kind of hesitation, a lack of confidence, and also a lack of trust.

Sometimes I feel as if I'm an emissary, someone who has been given a mission. What this mission is, I don't know.

"CHECKED BY THE COMMITTEE," reads the entry in Hannah's agent file from November 14, 1943. "Found to be entirely suitable for the job, in fact the best candidate from her country."

A week later she's in training. Her target is the city of her birth, the setting and inspiration for her father's plays and stories, the very place she fled—Budapest.

IN A DOWNPOUR ONE DAY in early 1944, a new recruit arrives at one of the operation's unmarked offices in Tel Aviv, in a building that houses a Hebrew socialist newspaper. Like Hannah, Joel Palgi was born in Hungary and fled just in time, arriving in Palestine before the war began. He climbs to the top floor. Outside, rain sweeps the Bauhaus facades and runs down the new streets to the beach. The city is only thirty-five years old, named after a novel by Theodor Herzl.

This scene opens Joel's personal account of the mission, *A Great Wind Cometh*, written at the war's end and published in 1946. The memoir is one of the best sources on these events, even if Joel's writing can seem suspiciously cinematic at times, with elements of film noir. "I ascended the narrow stairs to a room on the roof," he writes. "An unfamiliar girl in the uniform of the Royal Air Force sat in a room cloaked with evening shadows." He lights a cigarette and looks her over.

Her hands rest on a table. Her "long, pretty legs are crossed." He registers that she's tall. According to her agent file, Hannah is five foot three—her stature seems to have grown in retrospect. "The blue-gray of her uniform complemented the light blue of her eyes," he writes, and on this the observer and the file agree. Her eyes were blue.

BUT ACCORDING TO THE biography for children *A Song of Light*, when Hannah arrives by sea in the fall of 1939, just as the war begins: "Her green eyes glowed with happiness as she carried her suitcase and typewriter down the stairs. She was here—in Palestine, land of all her hopes. In her new patent-leather shoes she gingerly stepped over the sea-water puddles along the wharf."

Still, I think her eyes were blue.

SHORTLY AFTER HANNAH'S NAME appears in the files in Tel Aviv, it shows up in the files at MI9 headquarters in Cairo—the late-colonial version of the city, traces of which are still visible beneath the overpowering Arab metropolis of the present. Soon she appears in Cairo in person, registered in the course for radio operators.

Some of the parachutists take cameras around Cairo like tourists, and their photographs survive. They show rooms with high ceilings, Egyptian sun pouring in through the windows; the Great Sphinx of Giza, the pyramids, the horizontal colossus of Ramses II lying

HANNAH

impassive behind smiling figures in British uniform. In the fierce light of these images, it's nearly possible to feel the blast of heat. I almost expect to glimpse Count Almásy of *The English Patient*, newly arrived in a biplane from the Western deserts. Hannah mails a postcard of the bust of Queen Nefertiti.

AFTER HER TRAINING ENDS by March, she's flown north across the Mediterranean to Bari to await her infiltration flight. Dafni, her partner for the jump, is with her, and Enzo accompanies them as escort, liaison to the British, and Italian translator. When I travel to Bari myself in pursuit of some trace of those days, I'm standing on the Corso Vittorio Emanuele II when a gust blows off the Adriatic and the palm trees on the boulevard begin waving their fronds like the hair of Medusa.

When she visited Italy before the war, the summer she turned sixteen, Hannah toured Milan and ascended to the top of the Duomo di Milano. "After taking the elevator up to the height of about 600 steps, I reached a stunning rooftop. All around were lacy, slender columns topped with statues, airy and delicate cornices—like a fairy-tale castle from a dream," she wrote. "It truly hurt my heart to come back down." But now Italy is ravaged, the ports bombed, the olive terraces sowed with mines. The Allies have liberated part of the country, but the Nazis are still fighting. Bari and other cities of the free zone are hungry and humiliated, debased further by corruption and crime, full of the displaced, of unrepentant fascists lying low, of armed men who may be communists or thugs or both, of soldiers from Michigan trying to buy girls with chocolate bars.

Enzo is still intoxicated to be back in his home country for the first time since the war began. He delights in showing his charges around the town, along the waterfront promenade, past the Teatro Petruzzelli with its great copper dome. Maybe they pass, as I did, the pier where fishermen sell the night's catch while drinking beer, flushed and boisterous by 10 a.m. One parachutist who arrives after Hannah records seeing a performance of *Rigoletto* while waiting for the infiltration flight; on a sign at the Teatro Petruzzelli eighty years later, the opera is still listed among the season's offerings.

"The marvelous daughter of a nobleman!" Enzo exclaims when young Italian women pass in the street. This is recorded by another of his charges that spring, who gives us his own reply: "Your aristocratic girls go about the city barefoot, selling themselves for a can of preserves."

Enzo doesn't laugh. He takes it personally. "This nation has been ruined by the fascists," he says, "but will be resurrected. It's a people of culture and art, one nearly as ancient as we are."

Despite their difference in age, sixteen years, Hannah and Enzo are kindred spirits. Unlike most of the others, they both came to Zionism from wealthy families and after rigorous European educations. They've read the same books. They both once believed in the promise of a future in which Jews would be equal citizens of liberal states, and both have seen the courses of their lives changed by the betrayal of this promise. The archive preserves a note in Hannah's handwriting that she begins by addressing Enzo by his last name—"Greetings to you Sereni!"—and begs him for books and newspapers.

HANNAH

The single biography of Enzo, *The Emissary* by Ruth Bondy, describes an incident a few years earlier when, as an envoy of the Zionist movement in Germany, a married father, he confessed his love to a very young woman, "a delicate blond girl of seventeen." She was startled, and the embarrassing matter progressed no further. Enzo is a man of strong emotion, far from his wife and three children. Hannah is unattached and innocent. But the records give no hint of anything similar here. Enzo, at this point in the story, is playing one of the roles in the classic hero's quest: the mentor, like Merlin in the Arthur legends or Athena in *The Odyssey*. The hero is Hannah. According to literary conventions, she must soon leave him and be cast out of the familiar world into one utterly different, where she will face peril alone. "During the quest," I once read in a book on heroism by two American psychologists influenced by the work of Joseph Campbell, "'ineffable realizations are experienced' and 'things that before had been mysterious are now fully understood.'"

As they wait near the airfield for the flight, Dafni listens to Hannah arguing with Enzo about the existence of God. "Enzo was an extremely astute man of great experience, a student of philosophy," he writes in his account of these days, "and he fervently postulated God's existence. Opposing him with clear, penetrating logic was 22-year-old Hannah."

ON THE NIGHT OF MARCH 11, 1944, Hannah is in a bomber approaching the drop zone, nearly immobilized by her jumpsuit and parachute. Dafni watches her from his position in the fuselage a few steps away. It's impossible to hear anything over the engines. Hannah is going first. It would be logical for her to be terrified, but that's not what Dafni remembers. "Her face glowed and she radiated cheer," he writes. "Below her parachutist's helmet her face seemed smaller, her expression almost childish, and her luminous grin reminded me of a little girl riding her first carousel."

These lines are written after the mission, when Hannah is invariably described as smiling and glowing, her eyes twinkling. I read this description not with disbelief but with skepticism. Even if she did appear precisely as described, it's worth remembering that she's a veteran of the amateur stage, the daughter of a theatrical family.

The red light comes on: Ready.

THERE'S AN INTERVIEW filmed many decades later in which Dafni calls Hannah "our Joan of Arc." People start calling her that right after the war, and it's not hard to understand why. The Hannah of legend is idealistic and prepared for sacrifice. If there's cynicism lurking somewhere in her character, it's well hidden. She's wedded to the cause. The times are dark and the Jews need a heroine, their own Virgin of Orléans. But in the interview with Dafni, when he says, "Joan of Arc," it's impossible to miss the sarcasm.

HANNAH

The parachutist is elderly by this time, past considerations of politics and ideology. The era of hagiography is over. He knew the real Hannah, not the myth. The myth tries his patience. So does the real person. She's stubborn and reckless. She may be too earnest for him, too obviously a product of refined education. Among the parachutists, she's not one of the boys. But she's as brave as they are, maybe braver. He respects her, he says in this interview, but doesn't like her.

WHEN THE RED LIGHT TURNS TO GREEN, she might remember the parting words from Enzo: "Remember, only he who *wants* to die dies!" These words are meant to inspire confidence, even if they are obviously untrue. Or maybe her thoughts are closer to the prayer of the Israeli Paratroopers Brigade, formed several years later: "Let it open above me, let it open!" If the parachute doesn't open, you're fated to be a "candle"—an image whose vivid nature suggests that it must have been coined by someone who actually saw the horror of a human hurtling toward the ground with an unopened chute.

The dark forest swings beneath her boots. The engines recede and the sky goes quiet. She's between heaven and earth.

THEN SHE'S SOMEWHERE in the wooded hills of northern Yugoslavia—at first the records allow no more precision than that. Eventually she's reported to be with the partisans of Tito's 10th Corps. Dafni is with her, but his account is shorter on place names than on descriptions of roaming "that beautiful land of mountains and forests beset by rebellion and battle, awed by the magnificent landscape." They see attacks and retreats and pitiful convoys of refugee carts, devastated villages and flames "devouring the work of generations."

In one poor village on the Yugoslavia-Hungary frontier, partisans surprised by a German attack slip down the hillside and hide behind rocks. Dafni and Hannah run after them as they retreat, the enemy firing down from surrounding hills. They pass groups of civilians stumbling away from the fighting with small children and emaciated cattle. The wounded scream and groan. Hannah catches up with Dafni, panting, and when they make it to the cover of the forest they collapse onto the ground just as a Wehrmacht platoon comes into view. Dafni's finger moves to his trigger.

"Don't shoot," Hannah says.

She's calm. "Her eyes," Dafni writes, "reminded me of what could have been forgotten in this nightmarish moment: Our goal is to rescue our brothers, and I can't let a hasty act of heroism endanger what is most important to us." The two parachutists keep still and let the Germans pass.

A similar incident occurs later in those months in the forest: A German patrol passes nearly close enough to step on the two of them as they hide. Dafni looks over and sees Hannah on her stomach, pistol ready, "a heavenly radiance in her eyes." A second parachutist who arrives later tells an almost identical story, one in which the hotheaded men are about to shoot when Hannah, the sole woman on the team, tells them to hold their fire to preserve their real mission.

HANNAH

. . .

Two months after the jump, Hannah's voice reappears for a moment in the files: "A few interesting and beautiful things have happened to me, but I must wait before I can tell you." Her correspondent is again her brother, Gyuri, who has now reached Palestine, and who knows simply that she's on a mission for the British. The letter must have been flown out of partisan territory by one of the light planes that came in and out with personnel and supplies. "My dear, I'm as worried about mother as you are, and it's a terrible feeling not to be able to help. Without knowing details, I can still imagine the situation is extremely difficult. You can imagine how much I think about you both, and more than ever about her."

Her orders, upon boarding the bomber in Italy, were to cross the frontier from Yugoslavia into Hungary on foot, then reach Budapest by train. Her commanders from MI9 want her to contact agents of British intelligence in the Hungarian capital, and her commanders from the Zionist movement want her to contact the imperiled Jews of the city. One of those Jews is her mother, Katherine.

At the time of Hannah's jump in March, Hungary is a Nazi satellite but still an independent state. The country's Jews are persecuted and alarmed, but they're alive, the last Jewish community on the continent of which this can be said after more than four years of killing. The border can still be crossed without undue difficulty. The plan is feasible when she leaps from the plane but falls apart as her feet touch the ground.

The very same week that she jumps, the Hungarian dictator, Admiral Horthy, is summoned from his palace in Budapest to meet Hitler at an Austrian castle, the Schlöss Klessheim. The Red Army is advancing from the east, and it's clear the Western Allies are about to open a new front in France. Hitler knows his ally Horthy is reading the map and thinking about changing sides. The ensuing scene appears in the memoir Horthy writes after the war, a book full of excuses and lacking in any reflection or penance, but nonetheless one with many scenes of drama and historical consequence.

When his special train arrives at Klessheim, the Hungarian considers taking his revolver to the meeting and possibly using it, or so he claims. He decides to spare Hitler because "justice was to be meted out to him by a higher tribunal." That's what Horthy writes after the war is over and his country is lost to the Soviets, when he's in exile in Portugal, and when he wants to be remembered as an opponent of the Nazis and not one of their dupes.

On the station platform, Hitler himself is waiting for Horthy with a few senior Nazis, including the army chief Keitel and the foreign minister Ribbentrop. The Führer appears older and more stooped than he was the last time they met.

The two leaders sit down to eat at the castle, joined only by a single interpreter. Hitler seems ill at ease. He mentions rumors about Hungary's treachery and threatens "precautionary measures." Horthy now grasps why he's been brought here, even if he still hasn't figured out that it's all a ruse. He objects loudly: He's a loyal ally, and Magyar honor would never permit him the underhanded abandonment of an alliance. The discussion becomes angry, but none of it matters, because the operation to occupy Hungary with eleven German divisions is already underway, and Horthy has been lured away from his capital only to ease the takeover.

Horthy moves for the door, intending to leave for the train station—but just then an alarm sounds and the castle is blanketed by a smoke screen. A Nazi official informs him that, regrettably, an air raid is taking place, and he must remain. No, he will not be able to place a call, Hitler's underlings apologize, as bombs have cut the phone lines. There's no bombing that he can hear.

It's a full day before he manages to return to Budapest, by which time police headquarters and the Hotel Astoria are full of Nazis and the newspapers have received a German communiqué announcing that the invasion was ordered by "mutual consent." German guards stand at the doors of Horthy's own palace. Though he remains in power, he has gone from ally to vassal. It is now that Adolf Eichmann of the SS moves into a commandeered villa on Apostol Street—one that still stands, with grinning, mustachioed Magyars carved into the wood pillars of the salon, and a balcony with a view over the Danube. In the lush garden outside, where today a door advertises a studio called Pilates Plus, a Jewish slave laborer is beaten to death in these months for picking and eating some cherries.

The legal persecution of Jews by Horthy's government and the old-fashioned antipathy common among Catholics and Magyar nationalists are now replaced by Nazi logistics. The system has been perfected across Europe. The country's eight hundred thousand Jews must wear the yellow star. In the provinces beyond Budapest, the Germans and their Hungarian collaborators begin "deportations," which the victims don't yet know is a euphemism.

Soon the trains to the special facilities the Germans have constructed in Poland are carrying twelve thousand people a day. In his memoir, Horthy claims that from his seat in the royal palace he is informed of the fate of his Jewish citizens only after most of them are dead.

Hannah learns of the full Nazi occupation of Hungary after her trek from the drop zone to the headquarters of one of Tito's sub-commanders in northern Yugoslavia. The border is now sealed. Her mother is trapped in Budapest with Eichmann and his lethal stacks of paper. Even if Hannah can somehow get into Hungary, movement there has become far more hazardous under Gestapo surveillance. Yugoslavia was meant to be only a way station, but now she's stuck.

This moment is when her companion Dafni sees Hannah burst into tears for the first and only time. But she doesn't give up on the plan.

THE MISSION FILES in Tel Aviv include a confidential message written by one of the partisan commissars that spring. The note is attached to a letter of introduction that the parachutists are meant to present—without reading it themselves—as they move among partisan units.

It's clear, Political Commissar Ivan H. Šibl warns his fellow officers, that the foreign parachutists want to get into Hungary "in any way possible." However, he writes, they must be denied access to any of the partisans' cross-border contacts. "Regarding intelligence about the enemy, we must help them as much as we can. At the same time, regarding the internal structure of our units or political or military councils, they should know nothing."

Because he's an officer of British intelligence, Dafni explains later, the partisans rely on his honor as an English gentleman when they entrust this note to him, believing that if he promises not to read it, he won't. But he's not actually English or a gentleman. Of course the parachutists read the note anyway, and also copy it and send it to their superiors, which is why it's in the files. The parachutists see this communication—perhaps ironically, considering how they came to read it—as damning proof of dishonesty on the part of their hosts.

The note ends with the partisan motto: "Death to fascism! Freedom to the people!"

The Jewish parachutists would love to see death to fascism and freedom to all people, including their own. But alas, alliances are never simple. The Yugoslav fighters are happy to have the canisters of modern weapons and the radio operators dropped by the British. But the partisans are communists, so they oppose capitalism and British imperialism and distrust emissaries of the empire. So, for that matter, do the parachutists sent from Palestine, who may be wearing British uniforms but are socialists themselves, readers of Marx who view their cause as the Jewish front in the global workers' revolution.

The parachutists learn quickly, however, that if they reveal their identities, their hosts become even more distrustful. True, these Jews may be enemies of capitalism and of the Nazis, but this doesn't make them friends. Not because they're Christ killers or baby murderers—communists are modern people who don't believe primitive stories. It's because the Jews are bankers and capitalist bloodsuckers. This was explained by Marx himself in his essay "On the Jewish Question." While Haim the Scythe is sheltered for a time in the house of a Slovenian farmer friendly to the partisans, he finds a 1944 almanac with the title *Calendarium*. Inside, he finds an illustration of a poor medieval peasant ploughing his field, carrying on his shoulders an exploitative nobleman. The next illustration updates the image for the twentieth century: A modern peasant carries a bureaucrat, who is carrying a bespectacled intellectual, and on top of all of them is a fat Jew, smoking a cigar and holding a wallet bursting with money. When a more educated fighter notices that these supposedly British parachutists speak English with strange accents, they learn that it's best to lie. Sometimes they say they're Welsh. The Yugoslav riflemen don't know any more about Wales than they do, and seem to believe their stories about longing for Cardiff.

"THE MEETING IS NEXT to the Catholic church in M.S. at precisely 12:00 and 17:00 as the bell tolls." This document in the archive, dated to those months in the Yugoslav forests, refers to an operation of the "quartet," one of whom is Hannah. Elsewhere in the same file there's an indication that the town of "M.S." is Murska Sobota, in Yugoslavia close to the Hungarian border. Hungary still exists today, but Yugoslavia fell apart in horrific fashion five decades after these events, so places that were in one country are now in another, a problem plaguing anyone trying to plot events of this war on a modern map. A few years ago, my father and I planned a trip to

Drohiczyn, the village in Poland where his mother was born, and where her parents and siblings were murdered by Germans in 1941 along with the rest of the local Jews. We booked a flight. Not long before we left, he discovered that there were actually two villages with the same name, and that we had the wrong one—my grandmother's village was now in Belarus. We never made it there.

Wherever the village "M.S." is, the clandestine rendezvous is to unfold as follows: "Our man stands with an unlit cigarette and asks for a light. The envoy from Group A answers: For you, I have one. After that our man answers: Thank you very much." It's unclear to me if the operation mentioned here is the planned infiltration into Hungary. The files are full of details that may not be significant but bring these days to life.

In another paper in the files, the commanders in Tel Aviv notice that someone named Michael has been "taking a special interest in Hannah Senesh." This Michael has now written several letters addressed to her, care of British headquarters, Cairo. Who is he? They're suspicious, worried that the mission's secrecy could be compromised. This is long before it becomes clear that the mission's secrecy has already been compromised—that it was compromised all along.

The note ends with a shrug. "It's possible," one of the commanders writes, "that he's just a young man who loves her."

3

BUDAPEST

In a bookstore on the Pest side of the Danube I pick up an illustrated copy of *A Martian's Guide to Budapest* and read it in my hotel room. I can almost imagine the city as it existed when Antal Szerb published his little book in 1935—a city of elaborate manners and ironic humor, teetering on the brink of modernity like a drunk on the railing of one of the bridges between Buda and Pest. Hannah was fourteen when this book came out. In the *Martian's Guide* an interplanetary visitor checks into the Hotel Bristol, brushes the stardust from his suit, and calls the author to ask for a tour. Szerb suggests a romantic walk with a woman across the Chain Bridge over the Danube, and then a walk back, "maybe with the same woman." Trying to imagine the city in these years, I cross the bridge, then cross back, by myself.

Other writers saw Budapest differently. Gyula Krúdy, for instance:

> *Often I think this city is like a cheap hotel in a back alley where the window shades are forever pulled down tight, never*

a loud word escapes into the night, the piano player has gone to bed long ago, the desk clerk is nodding off; but when the police raid the place they find a travelling salesman bricked into the wall, a woman choked to death by pillows and a small child squatting in the unused summer stove.

AT THE RÁKOSKERESZTÚR CEMETERY I visit the grave of Hannah's father, Béla, who died when he was just thirty-three. His work wasn't translated into English, and Hungarians inform me that he's not much remembered even in his own tongue. For conservative Catholics and nationalists, he was a degenerate polluter of Hungarian culture and a Jew. For the communists who came after the war, he was a bourgeois and a Jew. Like many Jewish writers in many countries, Béla imagined his home as something wittier and friendlier than it was. Maybe this was delusion, or maybe an attempt to create the world he wanted by sheer force of literary will. If he had a transcendent masterpiece in him, he didn't have time to write it. There are literary statues around Budapest—this is one of the city's best features—but not of Béla.

Walking past some cafés in Pest, for example, I encounter a bronze Miklós Radnóty, a writer who believed, like Antal Szerb, that conversion to Christianity meant he wasn't Jewish, and discovered too late that many others didn't agree. On the death march in 1944 he scribbled a little poem:

> *Shot through the nape. I whispered to myself,*
> *That's how you too will end.*

The paper was found on his body, perhaps with "earth and dried blood mingling in my ear," as he predicted. Shortly afterward, Szerb was killed in a work camp. At least Béla never knew the fate of his city and his colleagues.

When Hannah is sixteen, two years before she escapes, one of the great Budapest novels is published—Szerb's *Journey by Moonlight*. It's possible to check if Hannah read it, because she kept a notebook in which she wrote down every book she read from age twelve. This notebook survives, opening with a childish drawing of a flower over the name "Senesh Anna" in a child's careful script—last name first in the Hungarian style—and continuing over the course of a decade. She lists the books according to the author's family name in alphabetical order. Checking the *S* page I found, along with five plays by Shakespeare, thirteen works by Hannah's father, which she began as a child and continued to read for many years. It was the only way she could hear her father's voice. But there's no Szerb.

In *Journey by Moonlight* the main characters are lovers from Budapest on a disastrous honeymoon in Italy. In Siena and Rome, the groom, Mihály, is derailed by memories of his past—specifically a circle of high school friends around the theatrical, hypnotic, and possibly incestuous siblings Tamás and Eva Ulpius, who held court and staged amateur plays in an old mansion in Buda. The most brilliant of the friends is Ervin—high forehead, pale skin, fiery eyes—a Jewish boy who converts to Christianity.

The conversion comes about, the narrator explains, because Ervin finds beauty and magic in the life of the church and craves the austerity of faith. But that isn't all: "Ervin, like everyone else in the Ulpius house except me, was a role-player by nature." He's looking for a part that doesn't end when the play is over, one he can inhabit with his entire spirit, one into which he can dissolve his past self. Once he adopts the part of a fervent Christian, it deepens until there seems to be nothing left of who he was before. Ervin reappears late in the novel with a monk's cowl and the name Severinus.

Reading *Journey by Moonlight* while also reading Hannah's diaries, I have the impression that Ervin and Hannah could be cousins—intellectual Jews in the same grand, twisted city, longing to inhabit a world of high culture where their origins aren't held against them, indulging in literature and theater, looking for a costume and for a story to order their lives, maybe for a way out of a social order that they sense will never accept them as they are. While reading Szerb's novel I start thinking of Hannah, the Hebrew pioneer and fighter, as a character dreamed up by a different girl, the one who draws the flower on her booklist, "Senesh Anna."

A NEWLY ARRIVED PARACHUTIST in the Yugoslav forest finds that Hannah has changed. This is Joel, who admired her in the Tel Aviv office in the mission's early days.

"Her eyes no longer shone," he records. "She was cold, her reasoning sharp. She no longer trusted strangers." She accuses the Yugoslav partisans of misleading them, frustrating her chance to cross the border and reach Budapest. When she and Joel first met, she had only begun sensing the powers of her own character, but now "she had full control of them."

BUDAPEST

One night, Joel and Hannah leave the bonfire and walk in the forest. She confesses to inner turmoil. She knows the risk, but she's going to cross. It's better to die with a clear conscience than to return without trying, she says, and if she fails, at least the Jews in Nazi hands will hear of her attempt and draw comfort and courage. These may be pronouncements placed in her mouth later on, but to me they sound like Hannah.

The Gestapo and their Hungarian collaborators lurk at every border crossing and train station. But she won't stay in this purgatory any longer. Dafni, the senior member of the team of parachutists, tries to change her mind, but no one can change Hannah's mind. This quality seems impressive now but doesn't seem that way at the time, at least not to her male comrades, who record their exasperation.

Back at headquarters though, Enzo is on her side. Yes—she's difficult. He knows. But her comrades must never forget, he tells them, that she's an "unusual girl." Just as Hannah's mother is trapped in Budapest, his own family is in occupied Rome, their fates unknown. In such circumstances he too seems to think that reason doesn't hold all the answers, and he doesn't believe in waiting.

THREE MONTHS HAVE PASSED since the night Hannah jumped. It's June, the air is warm, and around the partisan camp at Kalnik the forests are lush.

Hannah's escort will be an escaped POW who does jobs for British intelligence—a man code-named Ivan, but who is French, and whose real name is Jacques Tissandier. The debriefing of Tissandier appears in the files, typed neatly in English.

The Frenchman is supposed to take a message to a British agent in Hungary, code name Achille, concealing the paper in one of his shoes. "MINI had warned me that, on my second trip, I should have to take a young girl into HUNGARY," he recounts in the transcript. Mini is Hannah. "After a day or two, she revealed that she herself was this young girl, and that she would come with me immediately because she had already been in Croatia for three months and did not want to wait any longer."

Two other men join the group, both Hungarian Jews who escaped into Yugoslavia and are now heading back to bring others out. The partisans promise to provide a guide for the four of them, but they drag their feet. As we know from the commissar's note, the one that the parachutists aren't supposed to read but do, Tito's men don't want to put their own frontier smuggling networks at the foreigners' disposal. Days pass. Hannah refuses to wait.

To reach Budapest she must trek four hours from the partisan camp, cross first the river Drava and then the Mura, reach a train station inside Hungary, and get a ticket to the capital without arousing suspicion. The Drava sounds like an obscure river, so I'm surprised when reading Hannah's diary to find this isn't her first crossing. In her former life before the war, at sixteen, she writes in her diary in the carriage of the train carrying her from Budapest to her vacation in Milan: "We're passing through eye-opening places, different in their nature from the Hungarian landscape. The Drava flows between hills that rise high and have little cottages clinging to their ribs." Now she'll be crossing at night, on foot, and will have to wade or swim.

The train station she must reach is at Mala Subotica. So it's possible that this town, and not Murska Sobota, is the "M.S." of the planned cloak-and-dagger rendezvous, the one with the smoking man outside the church. I can't be sure, but it makes sense, as the plan also refers to a "quartet," and there are four in Hannah's party. But unlike the first plan, this one doesn't involve a church, so maybe not.

They set out from the partisan camp in the evening with three armed partisans. Hannah carries a radio transmitter in a suitcase along with her MI9 codebook. She also has US dollars, Hungarian bills, and gold coins. It has been nearly five years since she set foot in the country of her birth. Their guides escort the party to the banks of the Drava. Hannah changes into civilian clothes, according to the Frenchman's report, hiding her blouse and beret but staying in military trousers. "We made the trip without hindrance until we came to the banks of the MURA," he writes. This river isn't wide, but it's deep. They waste precious time looking for a place to ford. The hours pass, and the sky goes perilously from black to gray.

Back at the partisan camp, her comrade Dafni is getting nervous by the time one of Hannah's escorts finally returns, a fighter named Maté. A full day has passed. The partisan didn't cross the border himself but says he watched from a distance and saw Hannah and her companions enter the railway station at Mala Subotica. Dafni radios the excellent news to headquarters. Maté didn't really see this, and it's not clear why he made it up. By the time anyone wants to ask him more about it, he's been killed in combat.

The partisan hands Dafni a note that Hannah wrote between the two rivers. There was a delay, it seems, because of a missed rendezvous with a smuggler. "It took five hours to get here," she has written, "and we made it all right, but as we no longer found the contact for the boat, we spent the day in concealment on the bank. In the evening we found the boat and are now on the far bank of the Drava." Some logistical arrangements follow.

Apart from this letter, I am sending you the belt, the gun, and the .33 cartridge.

Best wishes,
From Mini.
June 9
22.00 hrs.

This is Hannah's last communication.

4

HEADQUARTERS

In the logbook at MI9 in Cairo, Mini blinks out of existence. The effect on Tony Simonds is unclear.

What insight I have into the British commander comes mostly from an idiosyncratic and unpublished memoir, *Pieces of War*, which can be found in the archives of the Imperial War Museum in London. In its typewritten pages the officer remembers Hannah as remarkable, but she's just one of the remarkable characters in his charge at this time. There's Stampedakis, a Cretan escape-boat skipper ("Dressed like a pirate, looked like a pirate, and in another age would have been a pirate"), and Billie Neville, his unflappable aide ("blonde, Eton-cropped, with a monocle"), and many others. It's no surprise that the person in charge of the operation has literary tendencies—the proximity of espionage to literature has always been evident. Spymasters and novelists begin with the same question: What if . . . ? At the time of this story, Ian Fleming, creator of

James Bond, is doing wartime intelligence work, and so is Graham Greene. David Cornwell starts out as a real intelligence man after the war before turning to fiction under the name John le Carré.

Simonds's memories were set to paper in the early 1970s, on Cyprus, when the author was immobilized after a car crash. That draft was lost to fire during the Turkish invasion of the island in the summer of 1974, and a second draft was reconstituted from notes the following year. That draft was lost in a fire in his bedroom at the Headmaster's House in the English School, Nicosia, and the final version was completed in 1979. "I am confident that this book will afford many hours of Anger and Criticism to a number of Pedants and Middle East 'experts' who will have a happy time pointing out the frequent inaccuracies in spelling, timing, and in the relation of occurrences," writes Simonds in the introduction. "I am glad to extend them this opportunity; and only hope that they get as much pleasure from doing so, as I have had in so doing."

Tony Simonds—that is, Lt. Col. Anthony Simonds—arrived in Palestine a decade before this operation as a young lieutenant in the Royal Berkshire Regiment, then served as an intelligence officer during the Arab revolt that began in 1936. Jewish leaders in Palestine identified him as a friend. In the memoir, he links his sympathy for the Jewish plight to his discovery, near the location where his fellow officers kept their Ramle Vale hounds for the hunt, of a Jewish village called Ben Shemen. He was surprised to find that many inhabitants were parentless children rescued from the Nazis.

When the war began in Europe and through the first grim year of German victories, Simonds recalls, his Zionist contacts begged British authorities to let them form their own units and fight. They may have been furious with Britain for closing Palestine to Jewish refugees and condemning countless numbers to death, but there could be no question whose side the Jews were on. The Zionist leaders passed one of their first requests personally through Simonds. France had just fallen. The Americans were still neutral. Almost all of continental Europe was in Nazi hands and England "on her knees," he writes, when Ben-Gurion asked him to approach the British general in Palestine with an offer of an armored division of Jews.

"I had great difficulty persuading the General to even forward the offer," Simonds recounts, "but eventually it went forward with a very adverse comment and disapproval." His superiors feared antagonizing the Arab world by arming Jewish units, "a misguided and foolish policy which cost us dearly in lives and equipment, but one that had absolutely no effect on Arab opinion."

In the memos of the imperial bureaucracy, it's possible to find a different kind of objection. One document from the Foreign Office, for example, rules that there is "no reason why any special arrangement should be made for the recruitment of Jews, any more than for Scotchmen or bus-conductors or people with red hair." And there are professional assessments like this one, from Sir John Shuckburgh of the Colonial Office in 1940: "I am convinced that in their hearts they hate us and have always hated us; they hate all Gentiles." Simonds sees things differently, though he admits to "average British latent anti-Semitism." He respects the determination of the Zionist pioneers he's met at their remote farms and spartan outposts, and he sees the need for a Jewish state. But he also makes an observation more closely related to his own interests and that of British special operations: The British aren't much use in speaking foreign languages or passing as natives anywhere beyond their own island; Jews, however, "are the outstanding opposite."

At this time, most of the Zionists in Palestine are people native to occupied states in Europe. Whatever they think of the British Empire, they are willing to die to fight the people killing their families. And their chances of dying are high, because while any Allied soldier captured out of uniform can be shot as a spy, these people also risk being killed as Jews. Nonetheless, he writes, "It was from this vast reserve of potential agents that I wanted to obtain help to run Allies Service Escape Organisations."

In the more rarified halls of British power, some support this idea for their own reasons. One is Lord Moyne, the British minister of state for the Middle East. "The scheme would remove from Palestine a number of active and resourceful Jews, and their training need not take place in Palestine," he writes. "The chances of many of them returning in the future to give trouble in Palestine seem slight."

THE BRAINS ON THE JEWISH SIDE of the operation were formed by very different circumstances—study halls of Talmud and Hebrew Bible, the world of multilingual dissidents, revolutionaries and fugitives. Shaul Avigur, born Meyeroff, for example, who can credibly claim to be the father of Israeli intelligence later on. Or the legendary Israeli spy Reuven Shiloah, born Zaslansky, of whom it's said that he once got into a taxi, and when the driver asked where he wanted to go, he replied: "I can't tell you that."

In 1944, these men serve an office entrusted with organizing the clandestine refugee ships running the British naval blockade into Palestine. The office, part of the Zionist proto-government called the Jewish Agency, is known as the Organization for Illegal Immigration—Ha-Mossad le-Aliya Bet. In Hebrew, *mossad* means "institution" or "organization." The word *aliya*, "ascent," is the lovely term for Jewish immigration to Israel, one that bestows nobility on the abject fact of homelessness and flight. Because this "institution," and these men, will evolve just a few years later into Israel's famous foreign intelligence service, for simplicity's sake I'll use the name Mossad.

The Mossad ships tend to be leaky freighters bought on the cheap in Europe, refurbished in a hurry with hundreds of wooden bunks, crewed by foreign captains and by Jewish volunteers with more motivation than maritime skill. They are vehicles not only for bringing Jews to the Land of Israel, but for conveying the Jewish story to the world in dramatic fashion. This is a time when the Zionist movement knows how to build a powerful narrative for its own people and for others, a talent that will wither in subsequent decades as the State of Israel settles into reality and gains more of the ordinary kind of power.

Even more than the Zionist pioneers need people, they need an apathetic and preoccupied world to understand what is happening to Jews and why they need a state. Images of forlorn survivors in papers and newsreels generate sympathy for the subjects and hostility to Palestine's British rulers, who are seen callously turning away emaciated people using destroyers and police batons. Strength isn't sympathetic, as Israel itself will learn later on. The Mossad's tactic works if a ship makes it to shore, illustrating the Jews' determination to reach their homeland and delivering immigrants who can work and fight. But it also works if the refugees are caught and forced back with cameras running.

The climax of the maritime effort came after the war with the ship *Exodus 1947*, carrying more than forty-five hundred Holocaust survivors from camps in Germany. Rammed and boarded by the Royal Navy, *Exodus* was towed into port at Haifa before a crowd of thousands—including several members of the United Nations commission deciding in those months whether to partition Palestine into Jewish and Arab states. The Zionists were desperate for this resolution to pass, while the Arab side was in vehement opposition.

The refugees were forcibly unloaded by troops, along with the bodies of three who survived the Nazis only to die resisting the British boarding party. One woman was heard screaming "Dachau," the name of her concentration camp, as she was led away. They were all deported back to Germany, which seemed like a defeat. But the images shocked the press and the international observers on the pier. A few months later, in a great drama in New York in November 1947, the assembly of the United Nations voted for partition and sanctioned the creation of a Jewish state. The mission failed, and the story succeeded. The Mossad men running the ships, the same people behind the dispatch of the parachutists, may not leave high-spirited memoirs or go on to write novels. But they are masters of narrative.

. . .

AND YET—still amateurs at so much else.

During the months of the parachutists' mission in 1944, a small Mossad team works out of an office in the capital of neutral Turkey, on the eastern edge of Europe. Istanbul is the perfect setting for covert services trying to run communication routes into occupied countries, a city typically described as "swarming with diplomats, spies, refugees, and intelligence merchants."

The young man in charge of the Mossad office is Teddy Kollek, later the mayor of Jerusalem, a product of Vienna but usually described for some reason in French—raconteur, bon vivant. Kollek and his colleagues do what they can in occupied Europe, trying to grasp the direction of events. Many of the telegrams and letters in the files of the parachutists' mission originate in, or are routed through, the Istanbul office. The messages include the names of agents, their aliases, and the planned dates and locations of airdrops. Kollek and his team have messengers who can cross hostile borders and help arrange false certificates and connections behind enemy lines.

Among the intelligence merchants in Istanbul are Americans, operatives from the Office of Strategic Services, the proto-CIA, who set up shop here after their country finally joins the war. They too need lines of communication into Nazi Europe, which requires people willing to risk their lives for ideology or cash. Such people are understandably hard to find, which is why the Americans are thrilled when a solution presents itself in the form of a Czech businessman who is eager to help. He has a roster of contacts able to run messages for payment. The Americans call their new network Dogwood.

One of the Dogwood couriers is a German named Scholz, a member of the German opposition to Hitler, who can traverse the route from Istanbul to Poland and back. Another is Bandi Grosz, identified as a Jewish convert to Catholicism and a smuggler of diamonds and carpets, known to the Americans as Agent Trillium. There's also an underworld figure from Budapest named Popescu—which fittingly is the name of a murky character from *The Third Man*, the 1949 film noir set in Vienna and based on the story by Graham Greene. There are others. The jaded hands of British intelligence in the city, as if in a Greene novel, know of the American network but keep their distance.

Fifty years after these events, the Israeli historian Tuvia Friling was conducting research at Oxford for his two-volume history *Arrows in the Dark*, now considered the authoritative account of what the Zionist movement did, or at least tried to do, to save Jews in the war. He was looking at the activities of the Zionist office in Istanbul. By this time, Dogwood had been known for years as a debacle of American intelligence. Of course the couriers were too good to be true. Of course they were all double agents. The network was run by the Abwehr, German military intelligence. Popescu was the German agent Erich Wehner. Agent Trillium worked not only for the Nazis but for the Hungarian secret police. And the trusted courier Scholz seems to have been none other than Lt. Col. Rudolf Scholz, commander of the Abwehr's Budapest station. The overeager American officer in charge in Istanbul was dismissed in disgrace.

What historian Friling figured out, by poring over lists of aliases, was that the trusted network of couriers used by the Jewish spies in Istanbul was the very same one the Americans used. The inexperienced Mossad men were approached by the same "businessman" and fell for the same German ruse. In the archive at Oxford, Friling told me, his hands began to shake. Like all Israelis his age, he grew up on the story of the parachutists and their secret mission. But this mission was never secret to the enemy.

In August 1944, for example, the mission files show the Mossad men in Cairo informing their counterparts in Istanbul that a new parachutist, Haviva Reick, is about to be dropped into the Nazi puppet state of Slovakia. The message includes her aliases, serial number, and the passwords she's meant to use: She's to say "Merhavia," the name of a kibbutz, and be answered with the name of another kibbutz, "Degania." The Cairo team asks Istanbul to get this message to their contact on the ground in Slovakia. The couriers who perform these tasks work for the Nazis.

There isn't a straight line visible between this revelation and what happens to the parachutists. We don't know, for example, if the alertness of gendarmes on the Yugoslavia-Hungary border precisely when Hannah crosses is because the Nazis expect an infiltration. This story does not have a Smiley or Karla as in a novel by le Carré. It's not a clash of spymasters, or even really a story of espionage. There are times when the Germans do seem forewarned. At other times, things appear to unravel by themselves.

5

ENZO

I travel to Rome to look for traces of Enzo, the mission commander, who was born in this city. Before I catch a flight from Tel Aviv I stop at the airport bookstore, where the English selection is for tourists. I see the following English titles next to each other on a table: *The Librarian of Auschwitz*, *The Boy Who Followed His Father into Auschwitz*, *The Fighter of Auschwitz*. Not long before, I happened to glance at a list of Amazon bestsellers in the category of Jewish Biographies & Memoirs and found *The Stable Boy of Auschwitz*, *The Daughter of Auschwitz*, *The Dressmaker of Auschwitz*, *The Redhead of Auschwitz*, and *The Happiest Man on Earth: The Beautiful Life of an Auschwitz Survivor*. There are many more, and also those where the *Auschwitz* is implied, like *The Boy in the Striped Pyjamas*. The name *Auschwitz* has appeal—the harsh foreign sound, the way it engages the whole mouth, the thrill of barbed wire and dogs. If *Auschwitz* is in the title, you can rest assured that the Jews in the book won't do anything disconcerting. At most, they will survive.

On the table at the airport there's Anne Frank, of course—people can't get enough of her. The book, the movie, the doll. She's a celebrity, an icon of adolescence, of migrants, of nonconformist sexuality, of the left, whatever victimhood is in fashion. Having lost her life to killers, her memory has now been seized to serve others. The private teenage naivete of her diary, which no one was ever meant to see, is retailed as generic wisdom. "I still believe, in spite of everything, that people are truly good at heart." At the Anne Frank House in Amsterdam, where Anne and her family were forced to live in hiding for fear of the Nazis and their many Dutch sympathizers, a staffer was ordered to remove his kippah not long ago because the apparatchiks who curate her memory saw this Jewish act as unacceptably tribal. The character Anne Frank isn't too Jewish, or religious, or strange. She does the right thing by dying quietly in a camp instead of disturbing the peace of Christians and Muslims.

Hannah and Enzo are the opposite of this.

ON VIA CESARE BALBO I find myself under the gaze of two Italian soldiers in battle dress. They stand with their rifles behind a metal barrier by a building across the street. I assume it's a sensitive installation, maybe a police station or government office, before drawing closer and seeing that it's just a synagogue—in fact, the very one in which Enzo celebrated his bar mitzvah at thirteen. The soldiers are here for the safety of worshippers, but the effect is to quarantine the synagogue, to cut it off from the normal life of the city. Even

ENZO

I, a regular frequenter of synagogues, hurry past. Across Western Europe this is how Jewish life, what's left of it, is conducted in our times. At the Great Synagogue on the Tiber, cameras ring the property, and the entrance resembles airport security. The doors of the cathedrals, churches, and chapels that fill the city of Rome, in contrast, are simply open—no one has anything to worry about, and you can just walk in.

I visit Enzo's high school, the Liceo Mamiani, where he met Ada, the strong-willed daughter of another old Roman Jewish family, whom he married. The school is a lovely building near a tramline running down a shady boulevard, accessed by ornate gates. On one of the stucco walls, in red paint, someone has sprayed "Free Palestine."

In his writing, some of which I have with me in my backpack, Enzo doesn't make much of hate. He doesn't seem to hate anyone, not even the Germans, and he doesn't expect anyone to hate him. Zionism is a positive vision for Enzo, not a response to animosity or a last resort. He will always call himself Italian, and unlike most of the characters in this book, he never changes his name to a Hebrew one. But for all his love of the country and the tongue of Dante Alighieri, by the time he turns twenty-two he sees his future somewhere else.

THE HOME WHERE ENZO GREW UP stood on Via Cavour, a short walk uphill from the Arch of Titus, with its engraved legionnaires plundering the Jerusalem Temple as they crush the last traces of the Jewish Revolt in the year 70 CE. Jewish kids in Rome used to dare

one another to run underneath the arch, which was thought to bring bad luck. The arch is still here—it has stood for two millennia—but Enzo's house is gone.

When Enzo is a young man in Rome, he dreams of writing the great novel that will capture the spirit of his Italian generation through the story of his family. The Serenis are pushed and pulled by contradictory forces—by their own ancient traditions, by secular liberation as promised in the revolution of Garibaldi, by the oppression of the Church, by the ghetto, Zionism, Communism, fascism. . . .

His father is a physician at the court of King Victor Emmanuel II. His brother Emilio Sereni becomes a communist, and at the time of our story is fighting with the red partisans in northern Italy. Emilio will later become a member of parliament. All of this certainly has the makings of a sprawling family novel. But the frantic events of Enzo's lifetime, as his biographer Ruth Bondy observes, force him from his desk and press him into other pursuits. He transforms himself from an intellectual into a Zionist farmer, organizes Jewish youth in Nazi Germany and Iraq for self-defense and emigration to Israel, authors a history of Italian fascism, raises three children to be at once Hebrew workers and Italians of high culture, and selects and commands the Jewish parachutists sent into Europe in 1944. There isn't much time left over. In the end, it's his niece who writes the novel—*Il gioco dei regni*, or The Game of Kingdoms, by Clara Sereni, published in Florence in 1993.

IT TAKES A WHILE for Enzo's colleagues in the Mossad to grasp what he's planning. At first they think he's just traveling to Bari to dispatch his charges at the airfield, arming them with the idea that "only he who *wants* to die dies," before returning to coordinate the mission from headquarters. But Enzo grew up in an eternal city where the heroic pose is incarnate everywhere, in marble, in the form of emperors and sword-wielding angels. How could such a man remain an administrator? One of his peers—Moshe Sharett, later Israel's second prime minister—will write: "Enzo was indeed one of the most dramatic figures in our movement, and became one of the tragic figures of the era." *Dramatic, movement, tragic, era*—these are words befitting Enzo. Not *coordinating* or *headquarters*.

In his memoir, the parachutist Joel remembers Enzo coming to the airfield to see him up the bomber's ladder as the younger man departs for the jump into Yugoslavia. They won't meet again. As they part, Enzo mentions the book he plans to write about the operation. Actually, Joel tells his superior, he's planning to write the book himself. It's he who will actually jump into Europe, after all—Enzo may be in charge, but he's staying behind.

No, Enzo insists. He will write the book.

Joel hugs the Italian as he climbs into the fuselage, laughs, and gives in—so he recounts in his book.

ENZO STAYS IN BARI. New parachutists, including several intended for infiltration into the Nazi puppet state in Slovakia, arrive in Cairo for training. One is Haviva Reick. In the target countries across the Adriatic, the mission proceeds. For a time, Enzo turns his attention to the fate of his extended family, looking around Bari for refugees from occupied Rome. He finds a few and gleans the first details of the destruction of the world of his family, describing it in a letter to Ada and their children on the kibbutz.

The SS came for the Jews of Rome on October 16, 1943, at 5:30 a.m., in the rain. "Since then no Jew openly appears on the streets; all remaining Jews are hiding in the homes of Christian friends, some of whom shelter them out of goodness and others for heavy payment." He is informed that members of the Sereni family were taken. Later it will be clear that more than one thousand were forced onto trucks that morning. The roundup took place in the shadow of the Vatican, where Pope Pius XII said and did nothing. Of the Roman Jews seized that day, only fifteen live to see the end of the war, one of them Settimia Spizzichino, a woman used for human experiments by Dr. Mengele and found at Bergen-Belsen asleep in a heap of corpses.

ACCORDING TO ONE ACCOUNT, Enzo chooses his own drop zone from a tourist map where he spots a place called Campo di Hanibale. If the great Carthaginian general camped there, he declares, it must be flat. I don't believe this story but can't resist repeating it. Another document puts the location near Ferrara, evoking not Hannibal but Giorgio Bassani, whose exquisite novel *The Garden of the Fintzi-Continis* tells how the war devours a family of Ferrara Jews whose daughter roams a walled garden with tennis courts.

Of course he will jump. To send Hannah and the others and not go himself—this would be a betrayal of the values that guide Enzo's life. Enzo is nearly forty, can't see without glasses, is slightly overweight, and has never used a parachute, but MI9 allows him a few practice jumps and he survives. Whatever his Mossad comrades do or do not know, his friend Simonds is clearly giving him what he wants. Enzo is in British uniform with the rank of captain. For a partner he's assigned a radio operator named del Turco, twenty-eight, formerly of the Italian Army.

Not long before, Enzo was still a pacifist, known at his kibbutz for refusing a rifle when on guard duty. He made do with a stick. He believed in peaceful relations between Jews and Arabs and among all people, and thought wars would end if everyone refused to fight. His final conversion happens, in his own account, in a suitably biblical landscape, on the road not to Damascus but to Cairo, traversing the thin highway through Sinai in a British truck. His hatred of bloodshed remains, he assures his reader and himself. So does his belief that violence will never bring peace. What the Nazis have changed is his faith that there exists no greater good than life.

Is it always true, he now wonders as the rumpled desolation rolls by, that "the call for such sacrifices is always a deception foisted by people with dark motives on naive idealists in order to use them as tools in the hands of evil and corrupt forces?" No, he sees now. There are causes worth dying for.

Some of Enzo's friends aren't surprised by his decision, even if they think it's irresponsible for a married man with three children. Enzo, in the words of one of these friends, understands Zionism as a personal journey toward a life of endeavor and meaning—"a revolution of the soul" and "a lever to lift the spirit of man." Over his years in the movement, this is the message Enzo brings to new arrivals in the Land of Israel, to his own children, to the skeptical friends back in Italy who still trust the goodwill of their neighbors and tell themselves things will work out. The natural response to darkness may be despondency, complaint, or self-delusion. But the correct response, the Zionist response, is action.

Ruth Bondy's biography of Enzo is called *The Emissary*. But someone who knew him observed that a better word would be "apostle." This is true. He may dream of a novel, but in the end the story he wants to tell is enacted, not written. This quality brings to mind another great Italian, Francis of Assisi: "You must preach the Gospel at all times, and when necessary use words."

When Enzo's comrades in Tel Aviv realize what he's up to, they do everything to stop him. They try to get him ordered back to Palestine, sending a message to Simonds claiming he's being urgently summoned home by his kibbutz. Enzo isn't fooled and writes an indignant response saying he's "hurt deeply"—"If something has happened to require my return, write what it is. If all you want to do is change my mind, you're wasting your time." He demands that his letter be shown to everyone involved in the operation, including Ben-Gurion himself. This is what people mean when they describe Enzo as "stormy."

If only he could have stopped Enzo, Ben-Gurion writes, he would have. "There was no replacement for Enzo. There wasn't another man like him." It seems strange that Ben-Gurion, the Zionist leader and future prime minister, can't influence one of his subordinates. But the Jews don't have a state yet, the Zionist hierarchy is fluid, and people don't do as they're told.

The British quartermaster in Bari issues Enzo a parachute, a pistol, and civilian clothes. Before takeoff there is a final note to Ben-Gurion and the other leaders back in Tel Aviv.

> *I'm going in the hope that I'll make some small contribution to our people and the war against Hitler. May we all meet again soon, and if not—goodbye to all of you, and thank you for what you have given me in this life, for the light I have seen in your light! Take care of my family if something happens to me.*

To the members of his kibbutz he writes that the drop zone is a place he's known since childhood, and that he believes Jews are hiding nearby. He knows how he's getting there but admits to uncertainty about how he'll return. He hopes to see them again. "And if not—and you know that I'm among those who think we must depart for such a mission knowing that only a miracle will get us back—I want you to know that my months of work with you were some of the happiest of my life."

When Enzo is in need of an incantation or prayer, as he certainly is at this moment, the text that seems to come to him most readily is *The Divine Comedy*. He can recite entire sections by heart and often does. In 1942, for example, while engaged in underground Zionist work in Iraq, he and another emissary were walking in the street in Baghdad when truckloads of Iraqi troops drove by shouting violent slogans against the Jews. This was not long after a Muslim pogrom in which several hundred Jews were murdered in the city, so the words aren't empty. The other envoy fell silent in dread. Enzo began reciting cantos from Dante.

ENZO

A reader of Primo Levi will remember the author carrying a vat of concentration camp soup hung from a pole, one end resting on his own withered shoulder, the other on that of the inmate Jean. This scene appears in *Survival in Auschwitz*. "Jean pays great attention," Levi writes, "and I begin slowly and accurately: *Then of that age-old fire the loftier horn/began to mutter and move, as a wavering flame.*"

Levi continues reciting the Canto of Ulysses, from the eighth circle of Dante's hell, to the part about "a mountain, gray/With distance, and so lofty and so steep," but then he stops. He can no longer go on to the next line. "Do not let me think of my mountains which used to show up against the dusk of evening as I returned by train from Milan to Turin!" he exclaims.

This scene takes place around the same time as our mission, in 1944. The fates of these two Italian men of letters, Enzo Sereni of Rome and Primo Levi of Turin, seem distant—one a free Jew, the other a numbered inmate in the Nazi camp system. But the lines will cross.

THE BRITISH PILOT flies Enzo and del Turco northward, over fascist territory, directly into an anticlimax. Fog blinds him and he reverses course, persevering through antiaircraft fire back to the airstrip at Bari, touching down near the cypresses on the beach with the two parachutists still on board.

They try again a week later, on the night of May 16. This time the sky is clear. Enzo jumps with the radioman, northern Italy spread beneath him, approaching slowly and then rushing toward his boots.

. . .

DEL TURCO LANDS IN A strong wind, rolls, hits his head, and blacks out. But the radioman has been lucky in the wind, the angle of descent, the precise spot where his feet touch ground. When he comes to, he can't see his partner. The fortifications aren't visible yet, and he doesn't understand how close they are to the enemy, though he will shortly hear the bugle call of reveille and hear the banging of tin pots as the Germans wake up.

For now it's quiet. He hears Enzo whistling, or thinks so, and follows the sound. But there's no sign of the older man, or of the canister with their radio. Now del Turco hears the military sounds, and when he peers over in the first hint of daylight, he sees that he's been dropped nearly atop an army camp. The installation belongs to the German Todt engineering detachment, though this becomes clear only later. He must get away. All he finds before he escapes—first reaching a farm where he procures civilian clothes, then making it to the road to Florence—is his partner's parachute, which Enzo clearly didn't have time to hide. There is no other clue.

From this moment all that's known about Enzo comes from others. He appears in glimpses—a flash here and there, like shell-bursts illuminating a stricken bomber at night.

THE FIRST FLASH is from Verona. An inmate at the old city prison, an Italian professor held on political charges, meets a newly arrived British captain who has been "severely tortured." This captain, the professor soon realizes, is in fact an Italian. At the end of August, the captain is taken from his cell and transported away with a dozen others.

The professor seems to be one of those who, caught up in the war, has decided that recording history, and particularly the names of people who may be erased, is an act of resistance. In a book of Italian classics that he keeps in his cell, he writes down the prisoner's name: Capt. Shmuel Barda.

Before the jump Enzo was offered a British alias but refused, instead choosing papers identifying him as a Jewish officer from Palestine. His reasoning is hard to understand. It's possible that while he knew his real name could endanger his family in occupied Italy, he couldn't bring himself to lie about being a Jew. This would be ignoble, and because he was circumcised, his Judaism would be apparent anyway.

I FOLLOW ENZO north on the rail line from Verona. The Alps rise in the distance but the land is still flat. As the train approaches the mountains the tracks begin to thread between crags, and out the window are scenes from fairy tales.

I've brought along the collected diaries and letters of Etty Hillesum and read them in my seat when I'm not admiring the view. "I want to get to know this century of ours inside and out. I feel it every day anew. I run my fingertips along the contours of our age. Or is that pure fiction?" Etty is a young woman of turbulent intelligence who lives under Nazi occupation in Amsterdam. She turns inward and lives more and more vigorously as reality darkens outside. She translates literature from Russian to Dutch. She embarks on a love affair with her charismatic psychologist, whose singular approach to analysis involves staging wrestling matches with his female patients. Like Enzo she dreams of writing a novel. Because I'm reading Etty while retracing the journey of Enzo, the two of them begin arguing in my head.

Her solution to her impossible situation, that of a Jew in Europe in the 1940s, is philosophical. Whether she's "within these four walls or within four other ones, what does it matter?" she writes. "The essential is somewhere else." But Enzo is political. He knows the walls matter. His solution is to act—he will build a state that can save people like poor Etty Hillesum.

"I don't much believe in help from the outside, nor do I count on it. On the English or the Americans or a revolution or God knows what," she writes. "No one should put his trust in that sort of help. Whatever happens is for the best. Goodnight." In the background, other Dutch Jews are being arrested and shipped to destinations unknown with the tacit compliance of most of their neighbors. Enzo, in contrast, not only believes in "help from the outside," but transforms himself into that help. Etty would find him backward, I think, maybe even comical, but she would be interested in him despite herself. He would find her infuriating but would also like her, maybe too much. Anyway, the philosophical approach is the one most people seem to find comforting these days. It's Anne Frank, a girl who expressed the belief that people are "truly good at heart," who becomes an international symbol, and not Hannah Senesh, who was eight years older, who knew that many people aren't good at all and tried to do something about it.

I don't know what Etty would write if she knew she'd soon be shipped to Auschwitz and killed at twenty-nine with her parents and brother. The force of her character and writing accompany me as Enzo and I approach the Alps and the border of the Reich.

ENZO

. . .

AT SABBIONARA a castle overlooks the houses of the town, which are hemmed in between the keep and the river. This part of Enzo's journey seems to be on a militarized passenger train with windows, and not in a freight car, so there's a chance he sees the towers and vineyards. The mountains of northern Italy are where Primo Levi is caught after a brief attempt to become a partisan. At the time of Enzo's journey his literary countryman is already at Auschwitz, watching the masses of Hungarian Jews arrive during the spring and summer of 1944, hoping his training as a chemist will be useful to the Germans and somehow spare him the fate of the new arrivals. "The worst survived, that is, the fittest," he observes, "the best all died." He writes this in a book I once bought at an excellent bookstore in Kraków, Massolit at Felicjanek 4, where I decided to go instead of visiting Auschwitz, which is a short drive away. All over Kraków the facility is advertised in signs offering local tour packages. "Kraków, Auschwitz, Enamel Factory & Wieliczka Salt Mine." No—I stayed away and instead read Primo Levi in the bookstore café with some Polish goths.

At Rovereto the valley widens as the train climbs. Past Trento, at dusk, the lights come on in the towns, and the sky becomes steely blue. The villages in the ascent to Bolzano have names in both Italian and German. Bolzano is also Bozen. I get off to spend the night. There's a ring of mountains above the rooftops and a cathedral tower of peculiar carved-stone latticework. In 1944 the Germans have a concentration camp nearby. The prisoners are herded off the train. Other people notice Enzo here, so for a moment he comes into focus again.

He's still in his British uniform but with two new insignia—a red triangle identifying him as a political prisoner and a yellow one that means he's a Jew. A prisoner named Ermanno Bellotti, who's been transferred to this camp from the jail of San Vittore in Milan, records that for a time Enzo is kept in isolation because he's considered dangerous. The guards can't have been worried about his physical abilities, but they may have noticed his charisma.

Also in the camp is a priest, Don Mauro Bonci. The priest leaves a record of meeting Enzo, noting his "inner peace." To keep up their spirits, the Jew and the Christian repeat Bible verses to each other. "He often surprised me," Don Mauro writes, "by his extensive knowledge of the Holy Scriptures which he could quote in Hebrew, Greek, and French."

On October 9, according to Bellotti's account, he, the priest, and Enzo are taken from the camp and loaded with a shipment of prisoners onto a train heading higher into the Alps. Now they're traveling in a cattle car. They climb northward toward the Reich frontier at the Brenner Pass.

They (and, eighty years later, I) pass the black steeple at the village of Klausen, then a red steeple at Scezze/Tschötsch, winding along the bank of the alpine river until evergreens appear. This is one of the most beautiful train journeys in the world, but it is invisible to them.

At the Brenner Pass, the beginning of the descent into Austria, the slope is so steep that the evergreens next to the track are visible only from mid-trunk, the bottoms far below and out of sight on my left. On my right, the rock face makes a dizzying climb toward the peak. Here the priest, Don Mauro, reports that "a deep depression seized them." They have left Italy.

Primo Levi also records this moment in his own journey to the concentration camp. "We passed the Brenner at midday of the second day and everyone stood up," he writes, "but no one said a word." Levi remembers wondering how many will live to see the return journey. Because he lives, he knows that of the forty-five people with him in the rail car, four will come back, and that of all the wagons in the train, his is the most fortunate.

The priest remembers Enzo emanating a kind of "contagious cheerfulness." But in the air of the Brenner Pass in autumn, with the weather getting colder, he must know he left a wife behind with three children and has accomplished nothing.

From the alpine pass his train route is the same as mine—first down through Innsbruck, then to the rail terminal at Munich, and from there to the suburban station where a sign reads "Dachau." From this little station it's a short bus ride for me to the camp. Enzo and the other inmates are marched here at gunpoint, then past the SS guardhouse and through the electrified wire.

ENZO REACHES DACHAU not long after Noor Khan, Agent Madeleine of the Special Operations Executive. Noor was thirty, a Londoner, daughter of a Sufi Muslim teacher from India and an American from New Mexico, and the author of *Twenty Jataka Tales*. She has no role in this story except to demonstrate that complicated identities and literary leanings aren't unique to the Cairo operation run by Simonds, or to his Jewish subordinates. Trained by F Section, the department responsible for sabotage in France, and inserted by airplane in the summer of 1943, Noor is captured. German counterintelligence then uses her transmitter and codes to mislead her handlers and lure several more agents to their deaths.

A few weeks before Enzo is marched through the gates of Dachau, the SS men shoot Noor Khan with three other women. Today there's a plaque in the crematorium with their names. Her handler in London was the famed British operator Vera Atkins, subject of the book *Spymistress*, actually a Jew from Romania named Vera Rosenberg. There is no end to these stories.

A MAN NAMED DAVID stands in inmate's pajamas by the double row of poplars running down the central yard of the concentration camp. The poplars are still here—not exactly the same ones, though, because the lifespan of a poplar turns out to be short, and new trees must be planted every so often to give Dachau the feeling of verisimilitude.

This David is twenty years old and both dead and alive, he records in testimony that appears in an anthology dedicated to the parachutists years later. Around him, skeletal prisoners run "like mice in a trap," and beyond them rise the guard towers. A friend from home sidles up to him. In the Hebrew they both learned in school, the friend imparts news: In this very camp is a *tsankhan* from the Land of Israel. This Hebrew word is a new one. In the Bible there is no word for parachutist. David doesn't know what it means, and his friend explains: "He came down to us from the sky."

ENZO

There are no further details of this apparition. David places the incident in March or April 1945, which doesn't match the chronology. Maybe he's misremembering the date. Or maybe rumors of Enzo circulate among the inmates even after he's gone.

6

HAVIVA

A few hours north of Tel Aviv, in a modest kibbutz archive, is a box, and in this box is a single Hebrew book. The book, *Members of the Kibbutz*, has been meticulously repaired, many of its pages having rotted during the months it spent buried in a Slovak forest.

The Hebrew word for "members," *haverot*, is the feminine form and refers only to women. In this collection of essays from the 1940s, workers and pioneers try to make sense of their lives in the chaos of Europe and the Land of Israel. The women write in the stilted Hebrew of the time, when the language was returning from the synagogue to everyday use but was still the mother tongue of nearly no one. There is no English translation, and even in Hebrew copies of this book are hard to find.

The place described in its pages is almost unrecognizable from the country where I live now. When Haviva is at this kibbutz—called Maanit, or "furrow"—working in the kitchen, suffering from rashes, from loneliness, and from the malicious gossip of the real-life members of the kibbutz, the impoverished commune is discussing the idea of building a little workshop to make glucose. The factory now towers by the gate and was recently sold for nearly $100 million. At Hannah's kibbutz, Sdot Yam, "fields of the sea," her comrades once sat in their tents dreaming of a fishing cooperative. Eventually they opened a marble business that by 2015 was worth $2.5 billion. Today Sdot Yam has a center for aquatic sports and a surf store, and the once-empty dunes nearby house a giant electricity station that powers our servers, Teslas, and air raid sirens.

In *Members of the Kibbutz* there's an essay by a tiler, a member of a nine-woman cooperative working for a pittance at the port of Haifa. Another is credited simply to "A Dairywoman." One is titled, "How I learned shoemaking." There's a poem about the miseries of life in a tent, the standard quarters of those days, when even couples had to share space with others. One essay describes a sunny day in the Beit She'an Valley:

> *The fields of Beit She'an are grooved with many paths. The expanse is planted with people and all roads lead to the "field." A deep joy in every heart. Happy in the feeling of shared fate that unites us all, we entered the small courtyard full of life and the bustle of workers.*

This is the sweltering valley where my wife grew up, the granddaughter of pioneers who battled malaria and mud to found her kibbutz. Most of the jubilance of shared fate had dissipated by the time she was born, but it's still a special place.

The people in the book are striving to better themselves. "One of the characteristics of the generation of revolution is the desire for truth and love," writes a pioneer named Yocheved Bat Rachel in a profile of four Zionist youth activists from Germany who died young. Although the volume is written entirely by women, two of this essay's subjects are men. She quotes one of the women, Aliza, writing in her journal, "I must make something of myself." One of the men, Ze'ev, puts it like this: "I promise (out of an optimism born of faith, or because there is no other way) that in the end the good in me will win." They wrestle with hatred, with the soil, with homesickness, with their own weakness. The figures in this book live according to examples from other books. Aliza compares herself to Annette, the hero of Romain Rolland's *The Soul Enchanted*. Ze'ev reads Trotsky's *My Life* and wonders if he could withstand the author's trials. All four of these young people cite, in their personal writing, the same line from *Jean-Christophe*, "Life is a tragedy, hooray!"

The women dream of becoming mothers. "The thrum of life trembles in their flesh," writes the essay's author, "and they know to listen to this sound as if to the strings of a harp. The call to bear a child, which arises from the depths of their souls, is not driven by sexual arousal. When the storm erupts, they open like flowers and open their hearts before a soul mate." At the same time, however, the members see marriage and the traditional family as bourgeois. The children of the kibbutz are to be raised communally and outside the home from infancy, in order to liberate their mothers for work. All of this is confusing for young women who must navigate the movement's new ideas while facing old biological facts. Elsewhere in *Members of the Kibbutz* the same writer, Bat Rachel, has a frank personal essay about the "erotic life" of the commune. "Sometimes I encounter light erotic expressions that are arousing, and they torture my soul," she writes. The connection between a male and female comrade, "even in a chance encounter," is understandable, but sex without commitment impairs the ability to find real love. The traditional home may be oppressive for women. But fleeting relationships contradict the need for a "deep and serious approach to the expressions of life."

In the case of the other parachutists, I have to wonder about the books that inspire them to jump. In Haviva's case I know it's *Members of the Kibbutz*, because she carries this volume in her pack from the kibbutz to Cairo, then over the Mediterranean to the airfield at Bari, across the Adriatic, then on the final retreat into the mountains of Slovakia, parting with it only at the very end, when she has no choice.

I FIND THE AGENT FILE for Haviva along with that of Hannah, in the archive in Tel Aviv. She appears as Marta (Haviva) Martinovic-Reick, height: 162 centimeters, weight: 62 kilograms, eyes: brown, hair: brown, citizenship: Czechoslovak.

When her file is created in late 1943 there is no country of that name, just as there isn't today. The Nazis have swallowed it, subsuming the Czech part directly into the Reich while leaving Slovakia to be run by one of their collaborators, the Catholic priest Tiso. After the war, Czechoslovakia will be reconstituted in the Russian orbit, only to split again with the Soviet collapse. Haviva's birthplace is in Slovakia.

Marta is her name at birth, and Haviva the Hebrew name she chose for herself, meaning "pleasant" or "beloved." Martinovic is the name of her not-quite-ex-husband, from whom she separated several years before the mission but whom she never bothered to divorce.

The Hebrew names of her parents, the agent file informs us, are Mordechai and Esther—the kind of detail that wouldn't seem credible in a novel, because these two names happen to belong to the two main characters in one of the great Jewish tales of double identity. In the Book of Esther, written down around the fourth century BCE, a young Jewish woman lives in Persia and has a Hebrew name, Hadassah, but goes by Esther, a Persian name. Her uncle, Mordechai, is a Jew of the tribe of Benjamin, but his name is also Persian. Esther's beauty wins her a place as consort in the royal court, where she's able to foil a murderous plot against the Jews of the Persian empire by the evil vizier Haman, who identifies them as a people who keep apart and wants them all killed. This book is read in synagogue every spring on the festival of Purim.

The ancient burlesque of Esther teaches that Jews have always had to maintain their own culture inside more powerful civilizations, making multiple identities a necessary part of their lives. The theme recurs in the stories of Joseph (who is also an Egyptian vizier named Zaphnath-Paaneah) and of Moses (a Hebrew who is also an Egyptian prince) and explains why Jewish people often have Hebrew names as well as names recognizable in the languages of

the cultures that surround them. The one on my birth certificate, for example, is Matthew. The possession of an identity with multiple facets, viewed with suspicion from the outside, can become fodder for accusations of disloyalty, of secret and subversive allegiances. This idea lies behind fantasies like the *Protocols of the Elders of Zion* and behind recurring plans for eradication, like the one enacted by Hitler in the years of this story, or like similar plans both older and more recent, detailed and defended in Latin, French, Russian, Polish, Arabic, and modern Persian, on parchment and online. These dark fantasies are the reason for the frequent demands that Jews be marked in some way, with special hats or badges, or that they be quarantined or boycotted. The Jews are not who they say they are. They're up to something heinous, and they're hiding it.

But for spies, multiple identities are a gift. Tony Simonds knows it. And this explains why the daughter of Mordechai and Esther—the Czechoslovak citizen Marta, aka the Hebrew pioneer Haviva, aka the MI9 radio operator Sgt. Ada Robinson—is about to be dropped back into the deadly place she escaped, and where the rest of her family has already been murdered.

HAVIVA'S AGENT FILE doesn't tell us everything. Nowhere does it reveal that her dissolute father abandoned the family when she was a child. Or that she grew up poor and living by her wits, working as a motorcycle messenger around the old spa town of Banská Bystrica on the River Hron.

The file does include the opinions of the men who interview her. On December 29, 1943, one writes that Haviva is "prepared to volunteer" and is "most certainly a candidate." Two months later, on February 27, someone else rules her "fitting."

One of Simonds's deputies at MI9, Squadron Leader Lawson, isn't sure. He leans toward approving her if better candidates don't turn up. But he "doesn't have full confidence in her as he does in Hannah S."

THERE'S A SCENE in Tel Aviv before Haviva leaves for Cairo, when she's seated in the truck about to set out on the drive across the desert. One of the comrades departing with her is Zvi Ben-Yaakov—tall, thick mustache, strong jaw. He's accompanied to the truck by his wife, Michal, who is pregnant and distraught.

Michal starts crying. Someone asks Zvi why he let her come to see him off in such a state. Wouldn't it have been kinder to leave her at home? He replies: Because I know I'll never see her again. When the driver pulls out and accelerates, the parachutists watch the distressed woman standing in the street until she disappears from view. Zvi's wife must worry not only about her husband's fate, but also about the woman with him in the truck. "Our way of life forces us to have a deep and serious approach to the expressions of life," reads the essay on eroticism in *Members of the Kibbutz*. "It can't accept the easy superficiality of bourgeois society." I'm not sure exactly how Haviva read that, but I'm sure she read it. No one, even her greatest admirers, would ever compare her to the Virgin of Orléans.

HAVIVA

. . .

HAVIVA'S LIFE SO FAR has been spent in rural Slovakia, then at an agricultural commune in the rough backwater of Palestine, with stints at militia encampments where she trained to fight and lead a squad. She has spent years in tents and barracks and has never seen a city like Cairo. Upon reaching the Egyptian capital and the custody of MI9, she's placed in the care of Billie Neville, the monocled and blonde Simonds protégé. Neville takes her to quarters in an apartment high above the metropolis.

"I'm writing you these lines from a very beautiful place, a grand room (sixth floor)," she reports in a letter to a friend. "Before me spreads a city illuminated in many colors. Cars rush back and forth." There's fine furniture in the apartment, a bird in a cage, and a dog who won't stop barking. She goes to the cabaret for the first time in her life, and to the Cairo zoo—"the world's fourth largest!" She notes the deafening noise of the streets. She sees the Great Sphinx. She climbs to the top of a pyramid and looks out at Cairo from the apex before jumping down from stone to stone like a deer. There's a photograph of her with other parachutists posing at Giza.

Her letters leave the impression of energy and restlessness. Before her departure she writes to Yitzhak Bergstein, a married militia commander with whom she had an affair—she wants to meet him before she leaves, he doesn't show up, and she's disheartened. There are letters to one of her fellow kibbutz members, Baruch, who is devoted to her and she to him, in her way—she regrets that she didn't have time to shore up their relationship before she left and thinks they may have a future after the war, even though he's also married to someone else. There are mentions of Haviva's ex-husband, the one she never divorced and who remains in the background.

Not long after she arrives in Cairo, she's in a soldiers' club when someone shouts her name. It's the bourgeois Arison, a complication from a few years back—they met harvesting grapes, and he fell in love with her. He wasn't married, but maybe worse, he was a capitalist. The family of this exploiter owned vineyards and even a car. In fact, the Arisons, businessmen and bankers, are still one of the wealthiest families in Israel. The politics of this man weren't acceptable to Haviva, a socialist, or to the austere members of her kibbutz, who frowned on capitalism and also frowned on Haviva, on her undisciplined approach to love and her cavalier approach to marriage—her own and those of others. The pioneers were supposed to be breaking the chains of the old ways, yes, but the proletarian Slovak went too far. Haviva ignored the criticism for as long as she cared to and broke it off with the capitalist when it suited her. The archivist who keeps her letters at the kibbutz, a woman who is eighty-three and grew up with people who knew Haviva, said most of them didn't like her. "Everyone here did what they had to," she told me, "and Haviva did what she wanted to." In the club in Cairo, Haviva speaks to her former suitor but lets it go no further than that.

The days are filled with British instructors who teach the recruits to operate radios and transmit in Morse code. They learn tricks of the trade from MI9's experts in evasion and disguise—the men, for example, are told to grow mustaches, because if you're on the run and need to look different in a hurry, it's much easier to shave a mustache than to grow one. The comprehensive history of the unit, *MI9: Escape and Evasion, 1939–1945*, to which Simonds contributed, mentions the instructor Jasper Maskelyne, "of the famous conjuring family whose sleight of hand had delighted thousands of people in the Britain of the 1920s and 1930s." Simonds apparently found the conjurer guarding an ammunition dump in Libya and put him in charge of teaching camouflage.

The classes leave Haviva exhausted in the evenings, unmoored in the overwhelming city. Her moods seem dangerously dark. "It happens often that I decide to go back to my room in the evening to rest, to sit with a book—but when I get there it seems that the whole room and its furnishings are falling on my head, and melancholy thoughts and longings fill my heart." She doesn't want to be alone, so she spends her waking hours with the other parachutists. But this leads to other problems, because of course the other parachutists are men.

The specific problem is Zvi, her partner in the mission to Slovakia, the one whose pregnant wife cried at their departure. "We're people with weaknesses," she writes to a confidante back home, Zipporah. An uninvited reader of this letter gets the impression that Zipporah knows all about these weaknesses. It turns out, Haviva writes, carefully omitting his name, that Zvi has been in love with her for some time despite being eight years younger and married. "Zipporah, I'm simply here and can't live without love. You'll understand me. This work requires me to make such great sacrifices, but why should I give up happiness? I can't say I love him, but he attracts me very much. As usual with me." The couple's attempt to hide what's going on adds to the strain. Haviva and Zvi are having trouble concentrating on their studies. Of course their comrades know.

A few paragraphs after describing her torment over the affair, she asks her friend to send regards to another of her men, the militia commander Bergstein. She's been writing him, she complains, but he doesn't write back. In another letter she mentions frequent messages from Baruch, the member of her kibbutz. She feels the need to explain herself: "I can't live without the feeling that I've left something behind."

Haviva seems determined and drifting. She's triangulating, using other people to figure out where she is.

In Cairo she turns thirty: "We're getting old, my girl," she writes. The men come over with red roses, a box of chocolates, and cigarettes. Age is beginning to weigh on her. She hasn't wasted her time but does have one regret: She doesn't have a child. She hopes she still has time, but "in the depths of my soul I sometimes hear a note of pessimism, particularly in the last few days." It may be a coincidence that this letter is dated two weeks after Hannah's disappearance on the Hungarian border. But I don't think so.

"My work requires optimism, great strength, and good nerves. Good nerves—I don't think I have these anymore, but I'm trying to control myself."

While Haviva is in Cairo in the summer of 1944, the Allied armies land at Normandy. Paris is liberated. The murder of the Jews of Hungary proceeds. The Russians advance. The awful heat saps her strength. She slumps into depressions that everyone notices.

As the date of the mission is set, postponed, and set again, the team frays into bickering at once furious and trivial. She finds solace in the company of the women who labor in the pages of *Members of the Kibbutz*. The days are tense, and at night the heat renders sleep impossible. Cairo, she writes, "is destroying us all."

By the end of August, most of the others have flown north for Bari and points beyond. Haviva and Zvi are among the last to leave. They're always together, and they grate on each other. He's a man of hard character, she writes. "In normal conditions, I know I wouldn't find this much patience for another person. But what can I do—fate has tied us together, in life and death, for a long stretch of time."

When Zvi is eventually sent ahead of her in September, Haviva sits down to compose a letter to his wife. The drama in this letter is unstated. Michal seems to have known, or at least guessed, and Haviva must suspect she knows. "You may wonder why I'm writing to you unexpectedly," she begins.

> *I would like to tell you something about Zvi that will make you very happy! A few days ago he moved on to his new work, where he'd long been planning to go. I've received good news of him, and I want you to be happy, as the news will soon reach you. Don't worry, Michal, take care of yourself and don't work too hard. Zvi is very concerned about you and will be happy the moment he returns to "you both." I hope that in a few days I'll meet him and we'll continue our work. I wish you all the best for*

the new year, and an easy time in the moments awaiting you. Be well, calm, and patient.

"The moments awaiting you"—this refers to Michal's impending childbirth. The "new year" refers to the Jewish calendar year beginning in the fall, around the time of this letter. Don't worry about your husband, I'll be with him soon. . . .

Haviva is a woman who can keep multiple truths in her head at once. In her biography, written by Tehila and Zeev Ofer, I learn that her lover's wife keeps this note "with mixed feelings" for the rest of her life.

HAVIVA FINALLY FLIES across the Mediterranean to Bari to await the drop. She has time to wander around the town, though Enzo is no longer here to serve as a guide or sing the praises of Italy's barefoot noblewomen.

On a wall in the Piazza Mercantile, over a restaurant and a recycling bin, I find a small stone relief of the Madonna and child. Because Haviva appears in her own writing as a woman attuned to detail, and one longing for motherhood, I think she notices this relief—that she stands here, where I stand, looking up at the two solemn faces. A few steps away, on an inner wall of the city's cathedral, is a fresco of the same mother and child in faded yellow and ocher. "We must parachute into Europe," Haviva writes, "like a mother breaking into a burning house to rescue her children."

It has been two years since she received a postcard from her own mother. One sentence: "We have been transferred to General

Government, formerly Poland." It says nothing else, only that contact will be possible through a post office box in Kraków, number 211. Deportees were forced to send such messages, and no contact will really be possible. The city of Kraków is the transit point for the Auschwitz-Birkenau camps, and her mother has already been gassed and incinerated, though Haviva doesn't know it yet. This is also true of her brother Imre and sister Franzi, and two-thirds of the Jews of Slovakia.

The Mossad men running the mission have an accurate picture of the events. By July 11, 1944, with Haviva still in Cairo, there's already a report in the files describing the mass deportation of Slovak Jews to Poland, about fifty-eight thousand people "sent mainly to Auschwitz, Birkenau and Lublin." The latter refers to the death camp Majdanek. Exceptions are made for doctors, engineers, agronomists, certain Slovak Jews with "important roles in industry and trade," and converts to Christianity before March 1939. Any Jew who has yet to be deported must wear a yellow star on the left side of the chest measuring twelve centimeters from point to point, and is prohibited from walking in the street between 6 p.m. and 8 a.m. Jewish homes must be marked, and Jews may not use telephones, cars, or radios, or walk on the street in groups. When walking alone they must proceed "with quick steps."

Two surviving Zionist activists in Bratislava, the Slovak capital, dispatch a panicked letter to their contacts in Palestine about places in Poland where "millions of Jews have been murdered and killed with asphyxiating gas." The writers beg the recipients to publicize it and "make noise worldwide." They still believe this will help. The month of their plea, April 1944, is the same month that inmates

Rudolf Vrba and Alfréd Wetzler, both Slovak Jews, escape from Auschwitz and publish the first description by insiders. The world has other priorities. The trains keep coming.

THERE ARE NOW four parachutists in Bari waiting to jump: Haviva, her lover Zvi, another agent named Rafi Reisz, and a familiar face—Haim the Scythe, the slight fighter who jumped into Yugoslavia vomiting at the beginning of this story. After months with the partisans, he's been extracted and returned to Bari. The southern infiltration routes into Hungary have been deemed too risky after the disappearance of Hannah and two other parachutists on the border. His new orders are to jump into Slovakia, to the north of Hungary, and try to cross from there. Rafi will accompany him. Haviva is to stay in Slovakia, along with Zvi, to extract Allied aircrew and help the British communicate with the local resistance in their role as MI9 agents, and find surviving Jews in their role as Zionist emissaries. The files reveal other plans to be executed if feasible: There are documents showing the various Slovak concentration camps, including a diagram of the Nováky camp on the River Nitra, and one document mentions a plan to blow up railway bridges if the collaborator regime begins new deportations. Haviva is ready to go when she's informed that she won't be allowed to.

It's a British decision. The MI9 commanders may be skittish because of Hannah's disappearance. Or it might be the revolt that has just erupted in Slovakia, led by two renegade generals trying to bring down the Nazi puppet regime. The rebellion means chaos on the ground, which increases the hazard of dropping agents from the air. The center of the revolt is Banská Bystrica, Haviva's hometown, now beset by Slovak fascist troops and German reinforcements moving in to crush the rebels. Haviva, who knows the territory and the people, is the ideal person to send. But the three men can go, MI9 says. Not her.

"We checked the situation here," writes one Mossad liaison in Cairo, "and found that in terms of the Partners' rules it's forbidden to send girls to carry out operations of this kind." The Partners are the British, and the problem seems to be dropping her "blind," that is, without resistance fighters on the ground to receive her, as Tito's partisans had awaited Hannah in the spring. "The danger of being captured is great, and a girl must not be among those caught." The Hebrew word I'm translating as "girl," *bahura*, can refer to a teenager or a very young woman; Haviva just turned thirty with cigarettes and intimations of mortality.

She has come all this way—passing the jump course, completing radio training, overcoming any doubts about her skills and unfavorable comparisons to Hannah. Haim the Scythe, observing this crisis as he waits for the jump, is surprised to see her burst into tears. "Her world seemed to have collapsed," he writes, "and she lost control of her nerves." The Mossad commanders try to calm her, addressing her directly in a dispatch: "Haviva, understand, there's no point in endangering a girl in this way." Yet the girl doesn't understand.

In another internal communication, the Mossad men name a male parachutist to replace her. But they add that "efforts must be made to find a way for Haviva, because we can't afford to lose her." Two days later there's another meeting of the men in charge, and yet another Mossad commander weighs in. He's heard that the Russians are dropping women fighters by parachute into the Slovak forests, and if that's true, there's no reason Haviva can't jump. Another commander agrees. "There's no rule that says not to use women in combat operations," he says. "Haviva can withstand any interrogation."

But when the bomber finally takes off on the night of September 14, Haviva isn't on it. She's still safe and stewing on the ground in Italy just after midnight when her three comrades jump hundreds of miles away, the pilot aiming for a drop site atop Mount Krížna in the Slovak hill country. In a house on the outskirts of a nearby village they're to find a schoolteacher who's with the resistance. They'll ask, "Has Karl arrived?" She's to answer, "He's not here, and won't be back until Sunday." The teacher will then take them to the rebel headquarters at Banská Bystrica.

The pilot lands the bomber safely back at the airfield and reports that all went according to plan. This is when Haviva writes her note to Zvi's wife with assurances that he's well. But she doesn't really know. They jumped with a radio, but no transmission arrives.

Three days pass. Haviva is despondent, at loose ends, when she's urgently summoned to the airfield. On the tarmac rests a silver monster from America—a B-17 Flying Fortress. The Americans are joining operations with the British and Soviets to aid the Slovak rebels, hoping their enclave can hold out until liberation by the advancing Red Army. This flight is going in with supplies and a team of American intelligence men from the Office of Strategic Services. There's also a journalist, Joseph Morton of the Associated Press, originally from the Omaha bureau, traveling with the OSS men. He'll be caught with some of them by Nazi troops and executed.

HAVIVA

There's room on the plane for Haviva, who won't need a parachute after all. The Flying Fortress will land inside the rebel enclave at the airstrip known as Tri Duby, "three oaks," a place she knows from childhood. It still exists today as a modest military field with a few Slovak Air Force jets by the runway. On the day she lands it's a dirt strip with several American bombers already on the ground, little Mustangs of the fighter escort circling in the sky above, a bustle of rebels and Allied troops in a variety of uniforms. She's in civilian clothes, with local currency concealed in her girdle and gold sovereigns in the heels of her pumps.

I DRIVE INTO BANSKÁ BYSTRICA. The Nazis are gone, the rebels are gone, even the communists are gone. Slovakia is a little state on the poor edge of the European Union, one that foreigners confuse with Slovenia. The highway follows the River Hron into town, wending between lush hills. Mist clings to the treetops. The skies are leaden.

This is a road Haviva often traveled on her motorcycle when she was young, and she knows the view. When they pass the hamlet of Kremnička she notices an alteration of the landscape: "an anti-tank ditch that was an unpleasant change to the scene she knew."

This last detail, which is foreshadowing, comes from the biography by Tehila and Zeev Ofer, the best source of information about Haviva. I'm not sure how the authors know what she notices. The biography is full of useful information, but it also (as the authors admit in their introduction) strays on occasion into imagining details for dramatic purposes. True or not, it's hard to resist this glimpse of the anti-tank ditch. So you heard it, but not from me.

Haviva has been away for five years. Anyone who has ever returned home after a long time away knows this unsettling feeling: You never left, and you're a stranger. When she enters Banská Bystrica she finds the main square, the same one she used to barrel through before the war, now full of soldiers and refugees. If you visit today you'll see the same two churches on the square, and the clock tower that is painted yellow and seems to lean slightly to the left.

Some of the townspeople must find her familiar. Doesn't she look like the fatherless Jewish girl with the motorcycle? But that was Marta Reick, and since then she's transformed herself into Haviva of the Land of Israel, and then into the British parachutist Sgt. Ada Robinson. She prays no one recognizes her, or if they do, that they're smart enough to keep it to themselves.

She expects to find her three comrades waiting—since they were dropped, Haim, Zvi, and Rafi have had more than enough time to reach the rebel capital and find the British military attaché as planned. But there's no trace of them.

It's thanks to Haim the Scythe that we know what happened, beginning with the jump from an altitude for which they'd never prepared, more than six thousand feet—"The huge black mass of the plane passed over my head, the whirlpool in its wake spinning me like a feather"—followed by relief when he's wrenched upward under an open canopy, and then an aerial view of a river that isn't supposed to be there.

He runs through what little he knows of the geography of Slovakia. Is it the Turiec? But that's nowhere near the drop zone.

Where, he wonders, is the clearing on Mount Krížna, and why is there a town beneath his feet? Only a fortuitous wind saves him from landing there, blowing him back over the woods.

In the distance, from his great height, he sees a burning village and the muzzle flash of artillery. A flare rockets up toward him, and he grips his pistol, as if this will help. The harsh light fades, darkness returns, and the ground rushes at him. He lands hard in low bushes and buries the parachute. When he whistles for his comrades the answer is a burst of gunfire from the trees.

The red tracer bullets arcing toward him mean that it's Germans, though it could also be partisans using German weapons. They're clearly trying to kill him, so it doesn't really matter. He sprints in the other direction until the gunfire stops, then curls up in a bush. He considers swallowing one of his methamphetamine pills, decides against it, and takes a swig from his gin flask instead. He's obviously nowhere near the target, so the map printed on his scarf is no use. He wonders if he's in Poland.

When he wakes up the sky is light. There's still no sign of the other two. Booms and thumps indicate that the battle he saw from the air is still going on. A mile away, across a river valley, is the unfamiliar town where he almost touched down.

A few flyers lie on the ground, printed on cheap pink paper—German propaganda leaflets, the kind dropped from planes. There's a caricature of Stalin shaking the hand of a Slovak soldier with one hand, while the Soviet dictator's other hand, hidden behind his back, holds a bloody axe. Behind Stalin is a rapacious Jewish commissar in the style of *Der Stürmer*, driving women and children with a whip. Haim relaxes. The writing on the flyer is Czech. He's not in Poland.

With his binoculars he looks across the valley at the mysterious town, making out a train station with a sign. He can pick out only the first and last letters, which are *V* and *Y*. This doesn't help, but later it becomes clear that the town is Vrútky, that the river is the Váh, and that he's in Slovakia, though in a different part of the rebel zone. The resistance forces are losing ground to the fascist counteroffensive, which explains the burning village.

It takes two days of wandering in the woods, avoiding German detachments and local peasants, but he finds first Zvi, then Rafi. Remembering what he learned from Tito's men—that the Germans stick to civilized valleys and fear the forested hills—they ascend higher into the Tatra mountains. It takes them a week on foot to reach the peak of Mount Krížna, where they were supposed to land.

On their trek, the three reach a simple cottage once built for hikers and mountain climbers, but now full of refugees fleeing the Nazi advance in the lowlands. Zvi, who was born in this country, speaks to them in Slovak, lying that he learned it from immigrant parents in London. The refugees are excited to meet British officers. The Jews say they're paratroopers forced to abandon a crippled aircraft, and the people seem to believe them.

There's a boy of about ten years old with blue eyes. Haim remembers his name: Ervin. The boy draws close to the airborne foreigners, touching their uniforms and weapons in wonder. "He thought us heroes from Jules Verne," Haim writes, "mysterious figures from the world of dreams."

Now from the trees comes Juraj Špitzer at the head of a troop of partisans. An entire book could be written about this Špitzer, and in fact was. He wrote it himself.

The parachutists have a short list of local contacts, Zionists who'd been active in the youth movements and were thought to still be alive. One of them is Špitzer, a member of the socialist-Zionist movement called the Young Guard, Hashomer Hatzair. And here he is, out of nowhere, a great stroke of luck. Špitzer will be thrilled to meet emissaries from the Land of Israel.

Zvi goes over to speak to him. Haim converses with a few of the ragged partisans until Zvi comes back with a strange expression. Špitzer is not happy to see them. He seems embarrassed. He spoke coolly and offered no help.

What has happened is that Špitzer has changed stories. He has abandoned socialist Zionism for pure communism and Stalin. He now utterly rejects his former ideology, and any form of Jewish particularism. He may have been born to Jews but doesn't feel part of the Jewish people. His nation is the proletariat.

In 1944, for a Jew in Slovakia who's been cut off from the outside world for years and has survived imprisonment, forced labor, and massacre, as Špitzer has, the idea of Zionism is impossibly distant while communism is concrete. Red partisan units are fighting the Nazis in the mountains, and the Red Army is approaching from the east. The communist solution to the Jewish problem—reject Judaism and seek equality in the Soviet project—seems plausible. The Zionist solution, which is to build a new country where Jews are the majority—this is a fantasy. To be a Zionist in 1944, or indeed at any point before the state of Israel is created, requires tremendous imagination, which is why the movement draws mainly the literary and the desperate.

The parachutists, emissaries from this fantasy, are crushed by Špitzer's change of heart. In a report to headquarters they convey their dismay at his transformation into a Soviet "collaborator." But they'll find that many have made the same choice.

After the war, it will seem that Špitzer chose wisely. He goes on to a career as an intellectual in communist Czechoslovakia through the 1950s and 1960s, editing magazines and writing for the cinema. His four screen-writing credits on IMDb include the World War II epic *Bílá oblaka*, set among the white peaks and wooden Slovak villages where he fought with the partisans, and where this part of our story is set. Špitzer also has an acting credit in the film, as "Bearded man."

He finds, however, that acceptance is elusive. Even under communism a Jew is suspected of strange allegiances, and it turns out that no contortions are enough. After the Soviet collapse, in his old age, he confronts the past in a sad little book that I've read. "I saw in assimilation a chance for the disappearance of anti-Semitism. Only later, much later, did I understand that persisting in the tradition of one's ancestors should not be a reason for persecution; the causes for persecution of the Jews lay somewhere else, in something different," he concludes. "Man must not be ashamed of his origin, only of his present." The title of the book is *I Did Not Want to Be a Jew*.

But though his memoir describes his war years at length, there is no mention at all of the three parachutists he met in the mountains, on whom he'd turned his back.

HAVIVA

. . .

NEARLY TWO WEEKS AFTER the jump, with everyone assuming the worst, the three missing men appear in Banská Bystrica, unshaven and filthy.

They're taken to the finest hotel in the old spa town, the Národný Dom, and given two rooms on the second floor. The British intelligence major attached to the rebels, Sehmer, wires his superiors: "A-Force Amsterdam turned up. Were dropped in Hun lines forty miles from pinpoint. All kit bar cash lost. All Jews."

Even in the midst of a war, the rooms at the Národný Dom are hung with expensive curtains, waiters glide through the dining hall in black suits, and room service is prompt. At this, the most glorious moment in the hotel's history, it is the nerve center of free Slovakia. The hotel has been commandeered by the anti-Nazi rebel commanders Golian and Viest, and the guest list reveals the international cast that has rushed here to help: envoys of the Czechoslovak government in exile from London, eager to assert their mostly imaginary authority; uniformed Soviets sniffing around their future sphere of influence; officers of the British and American armies, their optimism about this uprising misplaced, a mistake for which some will soon pay with their lives. There are also figures of uncertain identity and nationality, one of whom is Sgt. Ada Robinson, who says she's British but doesn't sound like it, and who wears a civilian dress, sunglasses, and a large hat.

I reach the Národný Dom after eight decades that have not been kind. Reviews on Tripadvisor describe what guests find (dirty wineglasses, unmade beds) and what they don't (air-conditioning, Wi-Fi, anyone at reception). But I'm just happy it's still here.

OUT OF THE SKY

When I arrive in the evening, the spies, officers, and politicians who once populated the grand dining room are nowhere to be seen—there are only chairs of 1980s vintage ringing empty tables in the darkness, and a grand piano of spectral white. At the reception desk is a vase of old flowers on a stool, a first aid kit on a radiator, and no one on duty. A kid who looks about nineteen, with a shifty look under shaggy bangs, squats outside the sliding doors. As I watch he's joined from inside the hotel by a friend with skin of unhealthy pallor and a black bathrobe, a teenage vampire. The Austro-Hungarian grandeur of the streets is still visible even though the light is nearly gone. The lethargic Hron flows by at the bottom of the street, in no hurry to make its rendezvous with the Danube near Esztergom.

Besides the television, have the rooms changed much? It's certainly the same high ceilings, the same windows looking across the streets Národná and Jána Cikkera. For most guests, the paucity of changes since the 1940s is less than ideal. But not for a visitor trying to imagine this place as it was in the war.

ACROSS THE RIVER the woods are the color of rust. It's nearly October. Haim replaces the water in the bathtub three times before he feels clean. Shaving hurts, but his cheeks emerge in the end. His uniform is taken to be laundered, leaving him no other clothes. In the next room he finds his two comrades using sheets as makeshift bathrobes. They eat an entire grilled goose and drink a bottle of champagne charged to the account of the Czechoslovak government in exile.

Haviva appears. Her eyes are invisible behind dark glasses, a green dress showing beneath her overcoat. They had no idea she was here—they thought she'd been left behind in Bari for good and didn't expect to see her again. They didn't know you could just land at an airfield and drive into town.

Do they consider, then, the obvious question: Why were they sent by parachute when they too could have simply flown here, as she did? Haim the Scythe comes across in his memoir, *Operation Amsterdam*, as a thoughtful observer. He's just been through two weeks of peril and exhaustion because of a navigation error. But if this question crosses his mind, he doesn't mention it. The daring of the jump is at the heart of who they are and how they'll be remembered—not as soldiers, or spies, but as parachutists. There may be easier ways to get somewhere. But that wasn't the point.

Several dramas follow on the second floor of the Národný Dom.

When the four parachutists convene, seated on the hotel beds, it's clear Haviva is their leader. She knows this town. She has already made contact with the local Jews who remain alive and has started organizing the refugees—about five thousand of them, by her estimate—who've escaped fascist territory into the rebel enclave. They've been sleeping in parks and under bridges, but with winter coming most have now found quarters with local families, or in the classrooms of the empty Jewish school. "By the time we found her," the three men report to headquarters, "she had set up an entire network."

Her new relief committee includes a local doctor named Tyroler, whose testimony survives: Part of their plan, he records, is to build bunkers in which Jews can hide until the liberators arrive. The parachutists also find a few escaped Allied prisoners waiting for evacuation, mostly Australians and New Zealanders, and some French deserters who somehow made it here and joined the rebels.

Haviva doesn't think she's been recognized. The danger is not just from Nazi sympathizers who hate Jews, but from communists who hate British imperialists and Zionists. She's hoping to be swallowed up in the strange crowd that has congregated in Banská Bystrica, all praying for the rebels' success. In the summer it seemed the uprising would prevail and that the Red Army would soon arrive, so the local Christians became friendlier to Jews. But now the Russian advance has stalled, the rebellion is faltering, and the fascists are closing in. "My situation is obviously quite critical," she writes. "We hope it will all end well. I live with only one thought—to save what can be saved."

These lines are from one of several letters composed by the parachutists at the hotel, then flown out from Tri Duby on the Allied aircraft maintaining contact with the outside world. "To write about all that I've lived over the last two weeks would mean writing a novel," Haviva tells her superiors, "and we'll leave that for when we get home, won't we?"

She goes by her mother's house, which is empty. She passes by her sister's pastry shop, thinking Franzi might somehow still be here, but finds strangers serving the cakes. They're all dead. Haviva knows that she's come too late. "Perhaps we could have stopped it," she writes. I wonder what she imagines she could have done.

HAVIVA

Haviva has set up her transmitter at a partisan safe house outside town, where she's been sleeping. She isn't planning to stay at the hotel with the three men, and after a few hours of exchanging stories at their first meeting she gets up to leave for a planned transmission to headquarters. But they don't want her to go. The British liaison has already reported their arrival to MI9, Rafi says with a grin, so tonight there's "radio silence," and a celebration of their reunion. She'll stay with them. But she doesn't have pajamas, she protests. Zvi, her lover, says, "This time you'll sleep like us, without pyjamas."

This is recounted by Haim in a tone of high-spirited adventure. Haviva is one of the boys, she doesn't mind. It's similar to the account from a man who was with Haviva in a militia training course a few years earlier, and who remembered spying on the women's tent through a hole in the canvas made with the tip of a pencil: "Every day we knew who was wearing white underwear with tassels and who was wearing simple pink ones." Or the account from another militiaman of the time they were out in boats in the waters off Caesarea and two of them "decided to play a joke on her" and got on board naked. Haviva pretended nothing was amiss, and the next day, before they set out on the boat again, she handed each of them a sock. Haviva is a woman in a complicated situation. I don't know what she really thought about any of this. But I do know she stays at the hotel, because that very night her safe house is raided by a German unit operating ahead of the regular army closing in on the town. The enemy soldiers capture or kill the partisans holed up there, and they seize Haviva's transmitter. Only the most unlikely providence has saved her.

News of the raid reaches the Národný Dom the next morning, and of course she can't go back now, so she moves in with the men. The only book she has with her is *Members of the Kibbutz*, and in nearly every letter to headquarters she begs for more. But it's too late. The free enclave is being strangled, and nothing will reach her.

HAIM AND RAFI aren't supposed to stay in Banská Bystrica but are meant to proceed as soon as possible to Budapest. It takes a while to figure out how best to get across the border between Slovakia and Hungary, and they're preoccupied with plans when, on October 15, they hear extraordinary news over the radio from the Hungarian capital.

For the second time, the Hungarian dictator Admiral Horthy, still nominally in power under German control, will try to outmaneuver his masters. For the second and final time he'll fail—in fact, this will be the last full day he will ever spend in his country. And for the second time, the setback will play out in the lives of the parachutists.

As on the day that spring when Hitler lured Horthy to the Austrian castle while the Wehrmacht moved into Hungary, here too we have an account from Horthy himself, from the memoir he published in exile. By now the war's outcome seems clear. What remains to be determined is only who will be around to see it. Horthy is desperate for a deal with the Western allies, the only way to spare Hungary the coming Russian retribution. Two weeks before, he'd sent one of his generals to the headquarters of the advancing British Army to ask for an armistice. But unfortunately for Horthy, his country is in the path of the Soviets. The British tell him to talk to Stalin.

In his memoir, describing how the Russians eventually ravage Budapest after all his machinations fail, Horthy calls them "hordes from the East" and "Asiatic barbarians." He loathes communists and doesn't want to talk to Stalin. But he swallows the humiliation. An agreement is initialed by October 11, with the Russians demanding his final assent to their terms no later than 8 a.m. on October 16. Horthy prepares a radio address for October 15, a Sunday, to inform the people of Hungary that their war is over.

The Germans move first. At dawn on the day of the scheduled broadcast, Horthy's adult son Miklós is invited to a meeting with covert envoys from Tito's Yugoslav partisans. But when the leader's son arrives at the appointed address on Eskü Square in Pest, there are no envoys. Instead, he's surrounded by fifteen Germans commanded by the SS thug Skorzeny, famous for his part in rescuing Mussolini from partisan hands the previous fall. The younger Horthy's bodyguards manage to kill one of the assailants before they're overwhelmed, their charge pummeled until he drops to the ground. The Germans roll the captive into a carpet and throw him in a van.

News of his son's abduction reaches Horthy just before 10 a.m., as he's about to meet his ministers at the palace above the Danube. He has already lost one son, a pilot shot down fighting on the German side in Russia. His living son has now been spirited to a waiting Luftwaffe plane en route to the concentration camp at Mauthausen, where he will live or die at Hitler's discretion.

But when the ministers finally convene, Horthy tells them he will still sue for peace with the Soviets. He sees no other way out. Chief of Staff Vörös offers a gloomy survey of the Red Army's advance: The forces of Marshal Tolbukhin are coming from the southern outskirts of Belgrade, and more Soviet formations are moving from Szeged and Debrecen. Budapest could be under direct Russian bombardment within days.

Now Hitler's envoy, Veesenmayer, arrives at the palace. Horthy protests his son's kidnapping with "great indignation," in his own words, and at first the Nazi claims to know nothing about it. Then Veesenmayer says the arrest is justified, because the younger Horthy, like the elder, has been conspiring with the enemy. Horthy must rescind his decision to surrender. The Hungarian refuses. Another Nazi envoy arrives, this time the ambassador Rahn, with a personal message from Hitler saying the same thing. Horthy tells his ministers that it's too late: "I have burned my boats."

By this time 1 p.m. has passed, and his proclamation has already been taken to the radio station and read on air. This is what the four parachutists hear, with disbelief and jubilation, in their hotel room in Banská Bystrica, just across Hungary's northern border. For Hungary, the war is over.

The streets outside the palace in Budapest are thrown into chaos. In the jails the news spreads, and some guards begin celebrating with political prisoners. A few inmates are released, while some prominent Hungarian fascists, members of the Nazi affiliate known as the Arrow Cross, are quickly locked up.

But the next move has already been planned, and now it's put into motion. German panzers clank into the streets and fan out. Arrow Cross and Wehrmacht men seize the radio station. A counter-proclamation is read on the air.

Units of the Hungarian Army in Budapest go over to the fascists. Now the radio broadcasts a speech from the Arrow Cross chief Szálasi, newly proclaimed as dictator of Hungary. The odious Szálasi fancies himself not just a leader in the mold of Hitler, but also a writer. He's at work, as Horthy tells us with disdain, on a book that will express his ideas of Magyar supremacy, along the lines of *Mein Kampf*, and plans to bestow it upon every couple that gets married in his new fascist state. The world can be grateful to the Red Army, and to the noose of the war crimes tribunal, for sparing us this book's publication.

Inside the royal palace, Horthy understands he's surrounded and orders his guards to stand down. Most obey, though one unit kills four Germans before being subdued. Before 6 a.m. the next day, the Nazi envoy Veesenmayer moves Horthy and his entourage, now prisoners, into two rooms at SS headquarters in a commandeered palace, where they are to await transport into the Reich. From an adjacent room at the palace Horthy hears a gunshot. One of his loyal officers, Lt. Col. Tost, who's been standing by a window overlooking the capital, lies bleeding on the floor, a suicide. The corridors are full of SS men, and one stays with Horthy in his chambers at all times. When Horthy pours a glass of water and takes out a pill, the guard lunges to snatch it from his hands.

Don't worry about Horthy. It's aspirin. He'll live to recount all of this in his memoir, in which he also describes himself making defiant speeches to the Nazis and complains about the food in the castle where they keep him for the rest of the war. His book devotes far less space to the murder of his Jewish citizens than it does to exotic dignitaries and hunting parties. In fact, he gives the mass murder the same amount of space as the following sentence: "To another Indian Prince, the Maharaja of Kapurthala, we owed the reintroduction of falconry."

IN THEIR ROOMS at the Národný Dom the parachutists hear the second proclamation from Budapest. So the war isn't over after all. Hungary is in fact more dangerous than ever, and the border crossing too risky. The planned infiltration is dropped. All four of them will remain here.

A new figure now appears at the hotel. Egon Roth is a bespectacled young intellectual, formerly an Orthodox Jew and now a fervent socialist and a Zionist leader. Egon escaped Bratislava, the capital, for the rebel enclave before the parachutists arrived and managed to get a few letters to his contacts in Palestine. These traveled, presumably, with the couriers running messages between Jews in occupied countries and the Zionist office in Istanbul—that is, the network of double agents run by the Abwehr. One of these is a desperate plea for help with false papers and passports.

"We're facing a situation in which we're forced to fight with our last strength for our simple survival," Egon writes. "And we're not far from despair; what can we do? How can we solve the burning questions advancing toward us every day with great speed?" The "burning questions" involve the correct steps to take once the Nazis and Slovak fascists arrive to finish off the surviving Jews. The word *burning* is less a metaphor than a description of what the enemy is doing to Slovak villages as they crush the revolt. More than ninety will be torched.

Egon is with the new arrivals on the hotel's second floor. Until now, the parachutists report, they've been greeted with amazement and joy by the Jews they've met. They're seen to bring hope, if not of immediate rescue then at least of a different future. But this isn't what Egon thinks.

The four parachutists are seated on the beds. Egon stands. His eyes burn behind thick lenses—this is Haim's description. "Why did you come here?" he demands. "Did you think this was child's play? Did you want to be heroes? Spies? What for?" He's shaking in anger.

Haviva tries to calm him. They knew each other before the war, before she made it to Palestine in time and he didn't. She was his counselor in the youth movement, the Young Guard, where they used to pretend to be kibbutz pioneers, or play games of cops and robbers but with cruel British soldiers and plucky Jewish immigrants trying to reach the homeland. He silences her before she can speak. "You tell me about conscience and solidarity. . . . Nonsense! Fairy tales! Who called you? Who needs you?"

The parachutists are dumbfounded. "I'm not a child anymore, and you're not my counselor," he shouts at Haviva, and it seems worth printing the text as Haim records it:

> *These aren't the days of "Scouts" games in the youth movement. This time the "captives" are taken to extermination camps, and the "dead" are really dead. They're not laughing on the grass, but rotting. I've seen the worms in their congealed blood. You've come to play soldiers. We've learned to live in the shadow of death, to forge certificates, to run away, to steal*

another moment of life. We learned to pass our brothers as they're led to the slaughter and not bat an eyelash.

You brag about how you stand tall, as if you came here as representatives of some master race from the Land of Israel. You must know: We're not ashamed to hide and grovel, escape and sneak across borders in order to save one more Jew from this giant tomb. For years we've been grateful for every day that passes and have been planning tricks to move each of us one step closer to the Land of Israel, and suddenly a few "heroes" get up, get on a plane, and jump into the open grave.

He stops speaking as coughs wrack his feeble frame. Egon isn't well. His shoulders tremble, and his eyes are webbed with red veins. They've been terribly irresponsible, he says. They're a burden on people who already have more burdens than they can bear. They should leave on the next flight.

Whether this is an accurate transcript of Egon's speech is beside the point. When Haim the Scythe writes it in his memoir, he knows how the story will end very soon for almost everyone in the room. There is such heat in the words he ascribes to Egon that it must be Haim speaking too—the heroic parachutist inserting a heresy into his own myth. Their brave descent from the sky changes nothing. They've jumped into an open grave.

THE FIRST ENEMY UNITS reach the outskirts of Banská Bystrica, and the town descends into hysteria. Soldiers of the rebel army strip off their uniforms and try to escape as civilians. Their generals, Golian and Viest, move into the hills east of the town, hiding themselves and their men among loyal villagers. The British major, Sehmer, tries to escape the encirclement with a few other men, including another MI9 parachutist from Palestine, Abba Berdichev. They don't make it far before they're captured and shot.

The parachutists, holed up at the hotel with what remains of the rebel command, decide to radio a list of targets for Allied bombers to hit not just around the town but in it, no matter the consequences. But before they can transmit, there's an unnerving whine in the sky, growing in volume, and when Haim looks out the window he sees a Stuka in its dive, releasing a black dot before pulling up. The explosion shatters the room's window and blows the door off its hinges. The next bomb shakes plaster from the ceiling. The parachutists are racing down to the basement with other guests when a third bomb blows out the lobby window and lacerates some of the escapees.

The German planes own the sky. There's no sign of Soviet fighters and no more hope for liberation by the Red Army. The foreign officers in Banská Bystrica are burning so many secret documents that the drops of autumn rain are ash black when they hit the ground.

The commander of the small American detachment decides to move his men down the road to Brusno, a factory town still in rebel hands, and Haim goes with them to set up a new transmitting station. Before returning to his comrades, he spends the evening in a bar full of drunken Soviet officers listening to a few Roma musicians. A prostitute notices his British uniform and sits on his lap. She smells of sweat and sour wine. "You're a naughty boy," she says in English, revealing missing teeth behind painted lips. "You certainly weren't the Englishman in the plane that bombed my house. Tell them not to do it again." He pushes her away. At his feet, uniformed bodies lie unconscious. One of the musicians dances on a table brandishing a spherical object in his hand. It's a grenade.

The musician takes out the pin and keeps dancing. An armed Russian major shouts at him to put the pin back in, but the man is drunk, and the action requires arduous concentration. Everyone in the bar wants the British lieutenant, Harry Morris, to lead a round of "God Save the King." He demurs. No, he must! But Haim doesn't know the words.

THE LAST REPRESENTATIVE of the Czechoslovak government in exile flees the hotel on October 23.

The parachutists have decided on their own plan. As Zionists they recoil at the idea of trying to hide, or of subsuming themselves in the masses of Christian or communist partisans. They'll assemble a group of Jews and head for the forest, forming an independent fighting unit under their own command.

On a map, they identify a location in the wooded hills to the east, a trek uphill past the tiny hamlet of Pohronský Bukovec, where the rebel generals are hiding. After much pleading, the rebel fighters remaining at the hotel give the Jews five Russian submachine guns, and some Czechs contribute a crate of grenades.

Because it's Haviva who's operating on familiar territory, and she who has the important connections and the dominant personality, much of the plan is hers. She decides who comes with them and who gets left behind in the town to face the victorious fascists. "Who am I to serve as the angel of death?" she asks, in Haim's account.

"Fate is fickle," Rafi replies. "Our list of the living might lead the lucky chosen to the grave."

The parachutists transmit the location of the new camp to MI9 and plead for an airdrop of weapons and supplies.

There's no answer. The storm might be disrupting transmission. They're on their own.

IT'S RAINING as the four parachutists lead the little group out of Banská Bystrica and east along the River Hron. Past the fairy-tale castle Hrad L'upča on its outcropping, they turn north and follow a creek into the hills. Haviva has refused to select only the young and able, as some of the others wanted, so their group includes the middle-aged Dr. Tyroler and his wife, a local pharmacist and his wife, and several other upstanding members of the doomed Jewish community of the town. The rest are young and able to fight, at least in theory.

Egon is among them. He may have changed his mind about the emissaries. In a letter that seems to have been flown out of the enclave with a dispatch from the parachutists, Egon writes, "Our fate is bitter—and you have sent us new life."

The two dozen figures climbing the hills under the autumn trees in the downpour, some of them wearing respectable jackets and muddy dress shoes, are not exactly a Jewish army, even if Haim does describe them in grandiose terms: the first freedom fighters against the Nazis under Israeli command. The shingle-roofed cabins of Pohronský Bukovec, emerging through the rain and mist, remind him of black dwarves wearing red hats. One of the young members of the group, Hili, asks Haim when he thinks the rain will stop, and when they'll be able to live like normal people again.

"At home," Haim answers. He means not the youth's home in Slovakia, but in the Land of Israel. To keep up Hili's spirits, and his own, as they trudge upwards he describes the sun that shines in Israel even at this time of year, and the hot winds called *hamsin* that blow in from the Arabian desert. Look me up after the war, he says, and gives directions: Get off the bus by the orchards of Pardes Hanna, next to the kiosk owned by Birenbaum, and walk east through the fields past Kibbutz Mishmarot until you see a clump of shacks and tents. This is his kibbutz, Kfar Glikson. When Hili makes it, the parachutist promises, they'll sing songs around a bonfire and remember the cursed Slovak rain of October 1944. Hili will end up being left for dead in the forest with a stomach wound and will lose a leg. But he'll survive somehow and will reach Israel.

At the village they stop to sleep, taking refuge in a schoolhouse commandeered by the rebels. That night, Haim wakes up to the glow of fire and to furious argument. Zvi is standing over a blazing woodstove, throwing documents inside. Haviva stands opposite, hugging a book to her chest like a baby.

She must rid herself of anything unnecessary, Zvi is telling her: It's useless weight, when they need every ounce of strength, and a Hebrew book will incriminate her as a Jew if they're captured. He wants to burn *Members of the Kibbutz*. Haviva won't give it to him. The argument grows more heated as Haim watches. The substance is not Haviva's book but the agonized love affair between the two parachutists, with Zvi's wife far away and death very close.

Haim finally steps in and takes the book. He digs a hole among trees near the schoolhouse and buries it with Haviva's radio. He notes the location, by two bushes adjacent to a forest path, hoping he'll be able to recognize the spot in the future, if such a thing exists.

IN A CLEARING ON THE BANKS of the creek past the village, I stand at a war memorial in the unsubtle Soviet Bloc style, an upright concrete slab. On it is the name of the partisan detachment that fought here, Stalin-Yegorov. Nearby is a lone grave with a red star. All around are wildflowers and the creeping greenery of central Europe, the burbling of the creek, the chirping of at least three avian species. If all this life seems oppressive, like vines throttling a tree, it's not the fault of this place but of what I know about it. A short walk farther up the creek reveals a wooden shack with an earthen floor, a structure barely tall enough to stand in. It seems old enough to have been here when the parachutists built their camp.

There's a sketch of the site made by Haim, later copied and translated into English, probably by someone at MI9 trying to figure out what happened. The drawing may correspond to the place where I'm standing, or not, but it certainly wasn't far. The horizontal stick figures, a legend informs us, are "bodies of killed people."

THEY BUILD CRUDE SHELTERS, stretching canvas over poles and taking over an empty wooden hut. Haviva sets up a field kitchen

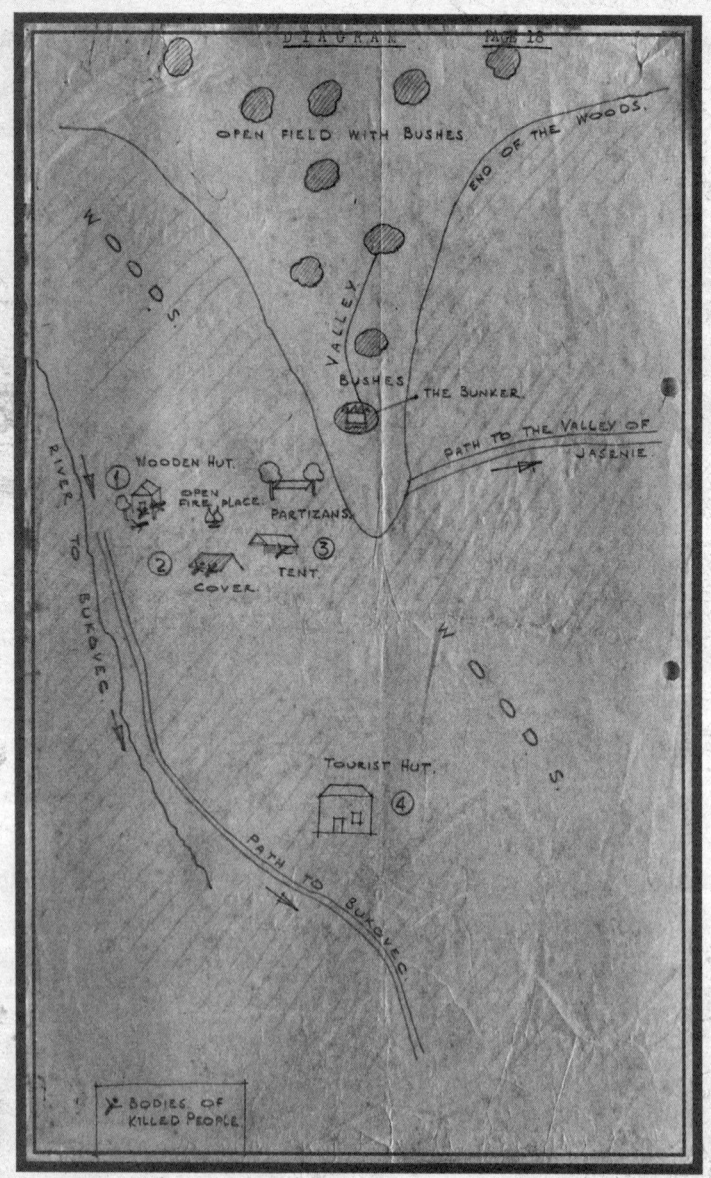

and organizes the women to run it. Haim, Zvi, and Rafi prepare the men for defense, giving away their British pistols and arming themselves with the Russian submachine guns. Some bring water from the creek and chop wood for a fire. Others hike back down to the village, ferrying more food up to the camp.

On October 28, Banská Bystrica finally falls. The swastika goes up in town and the Nazi puppet Tiso arrives in the square by the clock tower, awarding medals to German troops arrayed in rows. The hotel bar at the Národný Dom is still full, but now the officers are Nazis.

On October 30, Haviva returns from a supply run with a last sack of sugar on her back. The Jewish camp is standing.

That night, Haim records, he lies in one of the tents and falls asleep with his head resting on the submachine gun, the clip pressing into his neck.

AT 6 A.M. THE FIRST MEMBERS of the group wake up. Two brothers, Miki and Samuel Kreiner, are standing guard. Fog blankets the forest and the camp. There are a few accounts of what happens now, and they agree on the important details.

A young woman named Stefi Friedman walks over to the creek to wash, leaving her sister, Arzi, at the tents. The guard Samuel takes a pot and goes to fill it with creek water for coffee.

A minute or two later, Miki sees his brother running back without the pot, gesturing with his hands by his head. He's pantomiming the shape of a helmet. Among the trees, dark figures close in.

Before his brother has covered the ground, Miki shouts, "Germans!" and gunfire erupts from all around them. He loses sight of his brother and will never see him again. Stefi escapes into the trees, but her sister is cut down among the tents.

Dr. Tyroler leaps up to the sound of shooting. Next to him in his tent he sees his old friends, the pharmacist and his wife, holding hands on the ground. They came prepared and have already swallowed cyanide. Dr. Tyroler grabs his own wife by the hand and sprints through the fog for the trees, wearing only one shoe.

The first thing Haim sees when his eyes open is a horizontal line of bullet holes in the canvas above his head. He hears a grenade explode. Instead of exiting through the tent's door he tears through the back, followed by one of the other young men, Sanyo, who's hit by a burst in the chest and crumples.

From behind a stump a few dozen yards away, Dr. Tyroler watches the enemy soldiers move methodically through the camp. Later the survivors will report that the commanders are German but that the soldiers speak a language that sounds like Russian. The eyewitness accounts don't differentiate between Russian and Ukrainian and most agree that the soldiers are Ukrainian collaborators, except for one account that says they're Belarusian. Many Soviet conscripts have changed sides in German prison camps. Haim takes cover behind an uprooted tree. He cocks his weapon and aims it at some of the figures moving through the fog but doesn't fire. There are dozens of them, and he's alone.

When he feels sure the soldiers have gone, he returns cautiously to the tents. The pharmacist and his wife are on their backs, eyes open, staring blankly at the sky. Haim moves Sanyo's body, which has been thrown on a pile of supplies, and pockets a package of cheese triangles wrapped in foil.

Egon is lying in front of the hut. The frail body has no visible gunshot wound, but his face is badly bruised. His glasses are gone, and so are his shoes. Nearby is Arzi Friedman, whose sister was at the creek when the attack began. Her black hair stirs in the wind, her skin white on the green grass. The soldiers stripped her, and Haim covers her with an overcoat. There are a few other bodies around, but none of them is Haviva. The two other parachutists, Zvi and Rafi, have also disappeared.

IN THE NEXT HOURS and days small groups of them wander through the woods—returning to the camp and scattering, the Luftwaffe in the air, German soldiers burning villages nearby, artillery bombarding partisan strongholds higher in the mountains. In a hayloft in the village just downhill from the camp, the rebel generals Golian and Viest are captured and shot.

Some of the survivors want to fade back into the towns down in the valley and risk the German occupation. Others want to go in the other direction, upward, to reach the partisans. Haim decides to stay put. He's left with a single comrade, David, a young Slovak Jew. By the fifth day after the battle, they've dug a hole deep enough to sit in. They call it their grave.

The temperature is dropping, the ground beginning to freeze. Inside the grave they have one sleeping bag, a half sack of potatoes, and other supplies scrounged from the camp, including some sugar, tea leaves, and a little box of lard. They figure it's enough to keep them alive for a month on strict rations. They climb inside and pull a few scavenged planks over their heads. On one of them Haim pencils the date: November 4, 1944.

A FEW HOURS AFTER the attack, Dr. Tyroler retrieves his missing shoe from the ruins of the camp. In the forest nearby he meets the parachutist Zvi, and with a few other stragglers, they climb toward the ridgeline, hoping to get high enough before the Germans return. They have nothing but the clothes they're wearing and a few blankets. It's afternoon when Zvi hears voices through the trees. The language is not Slovak or German, but Russian.

The parachutist now makes a terrible mistake. Zvi hasn't understood the identity of the Nazi troops in this sector and assumes that Russian means friends—Soviet fighters with the red partisans. The parachutist, the doctor, and the others break into a run downhill toward the voices and safety. By the time they see the Nazi uniforms it's too late. They raise their hands.

The soldiers take the prisoners' weapons and anything else they have—watches, blankets, and money. They lead them at gunpoint to a nearby encampment and to the tent of the German commander, a Col. Wildner, where the captives are dealt their next shock: Haviva is here, holding the wounded Rafi in her arms. A bullet wound in his shoulder has been crudely dressed with his MI9 map scarf.

The German colonel personally questions the three captured parachutists and the eight other Jews caught with them. When he's done, he orders them taken up the hill. The soldiers force the prisoners to ascend the incline, arrange the victims in a line, and begin preparing their weapons. "In whispered exchanges," records the doctor, "we parted from one another."

Then the German colonel changes his mind. He marches them back downhill to the army camp, where he makes them stand at attention all night, shivering in the cold. In the morning they're herded down toward the valley. The Nazis now separate the uniformed parachutists, Haviva, Zvi, and Rafi, from the civilians and force the three of them into a car.

"My dear, I hope this won't be the last letter I write you."

Zvi is writing from a cell after weeks of Gestapo interrogation. He plans to give the letter to a Christian inmate who has a better chance of getting out. It's addressed to his wife, Michal, at their kibbutz on the shore of the Sea of Galilee. He knows she must be heavy with pregnancy by now, and sick with worry. The survival of this letter is miraculous, but here it is.

"I write sitting in a cell in the prison in Banská Bystrica, not knowing what tomorrow will bring. In any case, I'm writing you this letter so that if I don't make it back, you'll know how my mission ended, and so will our child who is to be born in a week or two."

He recounts how the British bomber dropped him off target; how he, Haim, and Rafi were greeted with machine gun fire, hid, then made their way through the battle zone with retreating partisans; how they found Haviva—a name that isn't easy for his wife, then or afterward.

They escaped the doomed rebel capital for the hills, Zvi goes on, lasting a week as the temperature fell. He describes how they were surprised by the dawn attack, how they fled into the fog, how Haim vanished. He recounts his fateful error in approaching the Russian-speaking soldiers.

By the time he and the other prisoners were marched down to the main German camp in the valley, the weather was clear and the fog had lifted. "To say 'brutal' would not be enough," he writes of the Germans. "I can't think of a word that would be. These are animals without human emotion." The enemy quickly discovered that his comrade Rafi was a Jew. Zvi doesn't explain how, but men were usually betrayed by circumcision. Haviva told them she was a Jew, he writes, which is startling—and here too we are left to wonder why.

Zvi, on the other hand, is claiming to be Christian. Is he not circumcised, or did he make up a story to explain his missing foreskin, inventing a medical reason, as some Jews were forced to do? He doesn't say, writing only that he's communicating with guards and prisoners in English, hoping they'll spare his life and send him to the relative safety of a POW camp.

Once the interrogators were done with him, he recounts, they threw him in a cell next to the one where Rafi and Haviva were held with six other Jews. The fact that they were British soldiers earned the two of them no special treatment. "On November 20 they took Rafi and Haviva and approximately 250 other Jews. They took all their blankets, and the cold was terrible. It snowed the whole time." Roma prisoners were taken on the same transport. No one came back. That's all he knows.

"Only two things are keeping me alive. 1. You and the child. 2. I must report everything my eyes have seen in this place."

It's time to finish. Maybe he's running out of paper. Maybe there's someone rapping on the bars.

He wonders if their baby is a son or daughter. He asks his wife not to mourn him for long. And he has one more request. "Please, don't let them make me a national hero, because what I did wasn't heroism," he writes. "It was only here that I saw we're too weak to be called heroes. This wasn't heroism. Anyone would have gone if he were asked to go, and I went because this is what the moment required."

BY THE TIME the letter reaches Michal, she has given birth to a daughter and her husband has been executed.

Somehow a letter from the wounded Rafi, imprisoned with Haviva in the cell next door, also survives.

It's November 19 when he writes. The next morning, he and Haviva are to be loaded onto a truck and taken down the road to the anti-tank ditch at Kremnička—the one that Haviva, according to her biography, noticed on her drive into town from the airfield. When I'm there, at the site of the mass grave in a field below the tree line, there's a rich smell of mud and vegetation. The ground is covered in strange brown slugs.

Rafi writes to his wife, who is caring for their baby daughter, Edna, and to the members of his kibbutz. He can't have much confidence that the letter will make it out of the prison and across the Mediterranean.

This isn't the first time he's saying goodbye—he's parted from them at every stage of the mission. But "this time it's much more serious," he writes. "All signs indicate that I've reached, if not my goal, then certainly the end of my life. This sounds so banal that despite everything, I must laugh." He has clearly been told what is to happen tomorrow.

> *It's good to know that I won't vanish from the world without a trace. I mean Edna, and your love for me. I ask for no monument beyond this feeling, and object to the idea of being made into a national hero. If anyone understands what happened here, it's me, and I know that this wasn't heroism at all. It always pained me to be admired too much, and I have the right to demand that my daughter know me as I really was, a man with all his mistakes and flaws.*

Don't make us into heroes. What else would heroes say?

OF THE THREE captured parachutists, two manage to smuggle letters out. What about Haviva?

In the files in Tel Aviv there's a report saying that a Slovak prison guard, a woman, is in possession of Haviva's parting letter. This is mentioned as a rumor, but I think it's likely—if her two comrades wrote letters, she did too. But none has ever surfaced.

7

THE MISSING

Most of the members of the mission on European soil are now missing.

The four in Slovakia were last seen fleeing to the hills, blinking out of contact amid the rebel collapse. In the fall of 1944, no one knows anything more. Enzo has been missing since he jumped in northern Italy, and Hannah has been missing since she crossed into Hungary. Two others who crossed ten days after Hannah are known to have been arrested by the Gestapo in Budapest, and it's unclear if they're alive.

At headquarters in Cairo, Simonds is saddened by this, though it's hard to determine the true emotion behind the jocular or deadpan facade of his writing. The Jewish parachutists are just one of many operations he's running, and his section is only one arm of MI9, which is itself a minute component of a vast war. In any case, direct control of the mission has now moved to a different officer, a

Wing Cmdr. Dennis, who doesn't have the same warm relationship with the Jewish agents and their commanders.

For the comrades of the missing parachutists, on the other hand, and for the Mossad men who recruited them, knew them, and feel responsible for them, the news is personal. They aren't hardened operators yet, and their dispatches are full of unprofessional expressions of grief. "Oh God! I will lose my mind from these reports!" writes one member of the mission. "If only I had lost an arm or a leg, or even a finger, if only I had spent a year in prison, if I'd been tortured for just one night—I would find it easier to bear the news."

A FRANTIC SEARCH for leads follows over the summer and into the fall. Some are grounds for optimism, and others are dark, but what nearly all share is that they're false.

After the disappearance of the four parachutists who led the little detachment into the Slovak forest, the commanders grasp at straws. "According to a broadcast from a station that seems to be American," reads one report, "members of the [foreign] delegations with the partisans survived. We assume our comrades are among them."

On the other hand, there's not much hope for Haim the Scythe. Civilian members of the group who survived the German attack in the forest saw the three other parachutists—Haviva, Zvi, and Rafi—alive in the confused hours that followed. But no one saw Haim. "The rumor says he was wounded and died," reads one Mossad dispatch. "I want to look further into the truth of the rumor, but tragically I believe it might be accurate."

There's news that Haviva and Rafi have been identified in a Slovak prison camp, either an official POW facility or a rougher holding arrangement for captured partisans: "They were undoubtedly caught with partisans." A subsequent report arriving via Switzerland places the two of them specifically in the Nováky prison camp.

A definite report arrives to say Haviva is alive. This is wonderful news. But the source acknowledges a chance that this is actually a sighting of another woman who was with her in the forest and who has an almost identical name, Aviva.

Regarding Enzo, missing since the spring, the British report in a telegram: "A-Force mission dropped Pratomagno two months ago landed on Todt fortifications." In other words, Enzo and his partner were dropped on top of a German military camp. This part is accurate. The radioman lost his radio but escaped, the telegram continues, and Enzo was arrested and shot. That last part isn't.

The British War Office, citing information from the Red Cross, reports that Enzo is being held at a POW camp in Germany, which is reassuring but also untrue. Another report says a Jewish chaplain with British forces has actually been in personal contact with Enzo, triggering a letter of relief from a different Jewish officer, Capt. M. Nahimson, to the chaplain: "I was happy to learn that Enzo is in touch with you, the more so that there were rather disquieting rumors about him." This letter is in the files, near a glum document reporting that this story has "proved false."

Another report arrives, reading as follows: "A telegram was received from Eldad, using his military name, saying he's well. It was impossible to tell from the telegram where he was." Eldad is one of Enzo's code names, but no one has actually seen this telegram. For a few months, Enzo's colleagues at MI9 and the Mossad assume he's a prisoner of war, and then, as the Red Army advances, that he's somewhere in the zone liberated by the Russians. Everyone knows the Soviets are slow to process and release foreign prisoners. But why isn't he getting a message through? It's possible, one of the intelligence men writes, that the Soviets are willing to pass on news of his condition but don't allow direct communication.

On October 18, Wing Cmdr. Dennis of MI9 reports that "information received leads us to think that Sereni was captured and shot."

This time the report seems solid. Tony Simonds isn't directly in charge anymore, but he writes solemnly to one of his Jewish counterparts: "Needless to say I wish to associate myself with W/Cdr Dennis' regret that so gallant a man has lost his life in the Allied cause, and I should also like to add my own deepest sympathy to Mrs. Sereni, and to all who honour and loved him, as I have also lost a personal friend in the passing of Sereni."

But Enzo isn't dead.

As time passes, the sources become more obscure. A member of Enzo's kibbutz reports that he heard from a man named Kalai, who heard from his daughter, who heard from a worker at the potash factory at Sodom, who—bear with me—heard a report on German radio saying Nazi forces in northern Italy are holding "one of the workers' leaders in the Land of Israel named Sereni." This absurd report is duly noted in the files. The intelligence men promise to find the person who apparently heard the radio broadcast, but unsurprisingly the lead evaporates.

As for Hannah—she has vanished without a trace.

Well, not exactly. There is a trace, one she left on purpose—a folded scrap of paper.

IN THE DIARY that Hannah keeps after arriving in Palestine, she writes that she has despaired of ever writing a poem in Hebrew. But then, a year into the world war and into her new life, she makes a first attempt. It begins,

> *In the bonfires of war, in the blaze, in the flame*
> *Between bloody seas that race,*
> *I light my little torch*
> *And seek a human face.*

It's not a good poem, but she's only learning the language. After that one from 1940, more and more Hebrew poems appear in a notebook that Hannah titles "Without Language," which she keeps along with her journal. Because she's trying to be a common laborer and is unsure of her control of Hebrew, she doesn't tell anyone what she's working on.

EIGHT DECADES AFTER these events took place, while I was writing this book, a war began a two-hour drive from my home with an attack from Gaza by Muslim gunmen who slaughtered, raped, and kidnapped many hundreds of Israelis living and farming by the border fence. The images seemed like ones from the parachutists' time, or from the time of their parents or grandparents—scenes that were not meant to recur after the Jewish revolt against history to which Hannah and her comrades devoted themselves, and that created a Jewish state and army.

A few weeks after the attack, as this army mobilized for a ground invasion, I happened to see a video of a battalion commander addressing his young troops before battle. The atmosphere in the country was one of fury, even biblical vengeance. But this officer, Lotem Faran, spoke differently. "War," he told his charges, "can bring a person down to the most basic instincts and urges: fear, cruelty, egotism, evil. It can take from us everything that makes us human.

"I want to read you a poem," he said, "written by a brave woman who was a poet and a farmer but who, when her people's fate hung in the balance, parachuted behind the lines of the Nazi enemy on a mission that had little chance of success, because she believed this was the right thing to do." He read them "In the Bonfires of War," by Hannah Senesh.

I think Hannah would be stirred by the masses of soldiers—Jews who don't need to wear British uniforms or beg colonial bureaucrats for space on airplanes. Hebrew is their mother tongue. They can pursue their enemies with jets and exploding air conditioners in the heart of Tehran. But she'd be surprised, not just by the survival of her halting lines of poetry, but by the war itself. This wasn't supposed to happen.

The parachutists hope that the creation of a Jewish state will be a solution to the problem—the hatred that has pursued Jews through the centuries and that has now incinerated the world they come from. They understand that an act of heroism is required.

They know that after the world war the Jews will have to fight their own war for independence. But they think this will be *the* war, the last one, not the beginning of an endless war in which their great-grandchildren will have to fight, a war that will wound them even if they win. They see the Middle East as a refuge, not as an insoluble new predicament. They jump out of the sky so that their children can stay on the ground, on their own ground, and grow pears or read a book.

When I came to Israel, five decades had passed since their mission. It was the 1990s, and I still thought that the country was the solution—that the strange animosity that persisted wherever Jews happened to gather was just a remnant of an evil past, that the ravings of racial obsessives, conspiracy theorists, and adherents of jihad would fade until they disappeared, that we'd eventually live like people anywhere else. I thought this through my own military service and through years of terrorist bombings in Jerusalem, including one at the cafeteria of my university, interpreting the attacks as the last gasps of the old world that we were leaving behind. I thought this despite a growing awareness that hundreds of millions of people, maybe billions, still see Jews as an urgent threat and the war against Jews as a priority. The hopefulness about the world that was built into the Zionist idea, we now know, was fanciful. Israel may be a bulwark against the problem for those of us who live here, a way to keep it at bay if we're vigilant. That is a revolution. But it's not a solution.

As this book progressed, my twin sons moved from tenth grade to eleventh and then to twelfth, and the date of their military draft approached. As I visited archives and conducted interviews, the son of the grocery store owner in my neighborhood was killed in Gaza with the military engineers, and the son of the bakery owner was killed in the paratroops. The son of friends was killed in his tank, and the son of other friends, who'd been kidnapped by Palestinian terrorists at a music festival, was murdered in a tunnel. My sons' former principal was searching a house in Gaza for a tunnel entrance when the booby-trapped structure exploded, and he died. My sons went to a half dozen funerals at the military cemetery and also went for their army physicals.

In 1944 the parachutists believe that you jump, hit the ground, and begin the historic change that's needed, the one that's coming. They're optimists. They don't imagine what we know—that you grip the sides of the door and jump, but when you land, fold your parachute, and lift your head, you're not on the ground. You're on another plane. And then you jump from that plane, hit the ground and roll, dust yourself off, and you see that it's just another plane. Ready? The light turns green.

A FEW HOURS BEFORE Hannah crosses the border into Nazi-occupied Hungary in the early summer of 1944, she's in the Yugoslav woods between the partisan camp and the frontier. With her is Dafni, the comrade who admires her but doesn't like her. When he describes the moment many years later in a filmed interview, he seems impatient with the twenty-two-year-old Hannah, and also with the way her myth swelled afterward to consume everything else about the mission and everyone else who took part. There's an incident, many years later, when the aging survivors and their families attend a commemoration at Hannah's kibbutz to find a sign celebrating them all as "Hannah and Her Comrades." It rankles.

On the forest path in Yugoslavia, Dafni thinks Hannah's desire to cross the border is reckless, but she doesn't care. Before the two parachutists part for good, Hannah extends her hand and squeezes his. He feels the paper in her palm.

This seems like a scene from a play or a novel, the kind Hannah reads and once hoped to write. Anyone of literary sensibility would appreciate it. But it doesn't work on Dafni. He's a practical man, not susceptible to the theatrical gesture. He finds it frivolous, even infuriating. He takes their mission at face value: They've come to rescue Jews and Allied airmen, and to fight with the partisans. They've been on the move for months with Tito's fighters, and they're on a hostile border. Hannah won't listen to reason and is walking into even more extreme peril. What the hell is this paper?

Send it to my kibbutz, she says. But when she walks off toward the border, and he stands there watching her go, he actually throws it away and leaves.

Afterward, when he calms down, he regrets his impulse and comes back. It takes him a while to find the paper, which is caught in the branches of a bush. When he unfolds it, he sees four Hebrew lines.

This is Hannah's second-most-famous poem. The words are soon intoned at meetings of Zionist youth movements and also put to martial music and recorded. In the movie *The Illegals*, filmed just three years later, in 1947, Jewish refugees trying to escape Europe can already be heard singing this song. As young Jews are forced to prepare for the war for Israel's independence in 1948, in which many thousands of them will die, the text is seen to have great meaning. The earnest style didn't age well. For a modern reader some effort is necessary to put cynicism aside and just listen to what she's saying.

> *Happy is the match that flared and lit the flames.*
> *Happy is the flame that burned secret in the deepest hearts.*
> *Happy is the heart that knew when in honor to stop.*
> *Happy is the match that flared and lit the flames.*

THIS POEM HAS SUFFERED from mistranslation. In the most familiar version in English, the first line reads,

> *Blessed is the match consumed in kindling flame.*

But the first word isn't "blessed." It's *ashrei*, which has no precise English translation, and is sometimes rendered "praiseworthy," but comes from the same Hebrew root as the word *osher*, which means "happiness." It's the word that opens a prayer recited several times a day in Jewish liturgy: "Happy are those who dwell in Your house."

The word *blessed* gives the poem a stilted tone that Hannah doesn't intend. She isn't distributing blessings but commenting on the state of mind of people like her, who are willing to die for a cause. A similar line opens an epic poem by Charles Péguy from 1914: "*Heureux ceux qui sont morts pour la terre charnelle,*" "Happy are those who die for the carnal earth."

Another problem with the translation is in the second part of the sentence, in which the match is "consumed in kindling flame." This misses what Hannah is trying to say, which is that the match *lights* the flame. This verb is the whole point of the poem. What separates the Diaspora from the Land of Israel, and Anna from Hannah, is action. This line of the poem lies at the center of the mission. In fact, I believe it's the key to the mystery that has always hovered around the events—what the mission was, and why figures who seemed to achieve so little became legends.

Decades after the operation, after the initial surge of hero worship in which Haviva became the name of a kibbutz and *Hannah Senesh* a 1958 production by Israel's national theater, questions began to be asked, cautiously at first, about why they were actually sent. A few historians pointed out that these war heroes seem not to have saved a single Jew or killed a single German.

A skit from the Israeli satire show *The Jews Are Coming*, in 2015:

A tough Jewish militia commander of the 1940s faces a briefing room. Behind him is a map of Europe marked with a swastika. A martial drumbeat sounds in the background. "Let's go, fellows," he says, shaking a combative fist. "Gird your loins and show them—defeat the Nazi enemy!"

The camera swivels. We see that there's only one other person in the room, a young woman in uniform. It's Hannah Senesh.

Hannah raises her hand. "Sorry, sir," she says with a puzzled expression. "But how will we defeat the Nazi enemy?"

"The plan," the commander declares, "is to parachute brave Jewish fighters into the Nazi front and then—to defeat them. So I wish you all the best of luck—"

Hannah interrupts again, raising her hand politely. "Excuse me, sir," she ventures. "I couldn't help but notice something."

"What?" asks the impatient officer.

"The Nazi army has hundreds of thousands of soldiers in Hungary, and we, on the other hand, are—"

"Yes?"

"One."

The commander pauses. It's true, he admits. "We're small—but we're smart and sneaky!"

"We?" asks Hannah.

OK, he concedes with a flicker of irritation. "You."

THE PIECES DON'T FIT TOGETHER—and for me, this is what kept these characters alive and unresolved for so long. There are straightforward tales of WWII heroism: Colditz, Omaha Beach, the assassination of Heydrich, the Dambusters. This story seems at first glance to belong on the same shelf, but it doesn't. What was it that the parachutists thought they were going to do?

Hannah's simple answer is written on the scrap of paper. She is going to light a flame in which she will be consumed. She doesn't think she's going to strike a death blow against Nazism or save the Jews. For her, the frontier that she's about to cross is in fact the border between life and death. She understands this, and she crosses anyway. She's happy to cross. This is what she says in the poem, which she knows could be her last message home. She was raised to take care with words. I believe her.

The scene in which Hannah presses her last message into her comrade's hand feels drawn from a book or play because Hannah grew up with books and plays. She's performing a role. She grasps what the real mission is. The parachutists aren't commandos. They're storytellers. They've been sent to write, with their lives, a Zionist story about the war—a story that will lead others not to despair but to action. In this story, Jews will be not victims but heroes. This won't change the war, but it will change how people remember the war, and therefore change the future. When faced with tragedy, those who know the parachutists' story won't pull the covers over their heads, or bemoan the cruelty of fate, or wait for someone else to do something. They will look out into the night, grip the sides of the door, and jump.

Of all the characters, it's Hannah who understands most intuitively what's needed, and it's she who is most adept at translating this expectation into action and words. Hannah is the symbol of the mission not because of her military achievements—she has none. But the mission isn't military, it's literary, and she's the best writer.

I'VE NEVER HEARD Hannah's voice. To the best of my knowledge, there is no one alive today who has. The closest I've come was unexpected—not long ago, through earbuds, while listening to a podcast.

The subject was the trial of Adolf Eichmann in 1961. Eichmann, who planned the murder of Hungary's Jews and millions of others, was kidnapped by Mossad agents from his refuge in Buenos Aires and brought to face justice in Jerusalem, and the hearings became a public exorcism in which Israelis finally confronted what happened in Europe. Zionists look ahead, not backward, and until this moment the events had been coated with euphemism, denial, and shame that Jews could ever have been so weak. Only sixteen years had passed since the war's end. There are things that simply can't be understood right away.

Among the first witnesses called by the prosecution was Zivia Lubetkin. This formidable woman was one of the leaders of the uprising in the Warsaw Ghetto in 1943. When the uprising came to its inevitable defeat at Nazi hands, she escaped through the sewers and survived to reach Israel, becoming an icon in a country that was determined to elevate instances of military bravery like hers. The day set aside for Holocaust memorial in Israel is called Remembrance Day for the Holocaust *and Heroism.*

In the courtroom, Eichmann was no longer the master of the commandeered villa in Budapest or the arbiter of life and death. He was a balding little man in a glass cube. In the old trial recording you hear the Israeli prosecutor ask Lubetkin to tell the court—and the masses listening live on the radio, and posterity—about her heroism. But her answer isn't what he supposes. She isn't interested in what he means by heroism in the Israeli state in 1961, by which time the Jews have a real army and a culture of military prowess. One of the barriers to understanding the story of Zivia Lubetkin, or that of the characters in this book, is the idea that they're Israeli, when at the time of their heroism there was no such thing. When she testified in 1961, Lubetkin was a citizen of Israel. In the distant future, her granddaughter would be the first woman to become an Israeli fighter pilot. But when Lubetkin performed her acts of heroism, in 1943, she was a

THE MISSING

Polish Jew in occupied Warsaw. "It was clear that we had no chance of winning in the military sense, or in the sense accepted today," I heard her tell the court in accented Hebrew, and I felt that I was hearing Hannah—an older version, looking back on the storm of events.

It didn't take her comrades in the ghetto long to understand the Nazi plan, Lubetkin said. It was "to humiliate us, oppress us, starve us, and, by closing the libraries, turn us into a nation of ignorant and uncultured slaves." In a discussion of the murder of millions, in the presence of one of the murderers, it's surprising to hear about libraries. But for her, this was the point. Even more than the Nazis sought physical annihilation, they sought to erase the humanity of their victims. And if this was the case, she said, "then our war is to preserve our humanity, to develop the spirit of rebellion against these decrees."

Zivia Lubetkin and the other commanders were counselors in Zionist youth movements, the same ones that shaped the parachutists and the generation that founded Israel. She was a socialist. She was twenty-nine at the time of the uprising, and younger people in the ghetto looked to her for guidance. She wanted the court to understand what she meant. "When I say *rebellion* I don't mean an armed rebellion," she said, "but action meant to guard the human, cultural, and social face of the youth."

LUBETKIN'S WORDS at the trial illuminated the story of the parachutists, and the way they understood their mission—that word containing not only the military meaning but the one it would have in an evangelistic faith.

Hannah's comrade Dafni, for example, remembers a night in the Yugoslav forest in the spring of 1944. There's a bonfire and ragged fighters, their rifles resting on the ground. This is before Hannah vanishes, so she's there, and so is a partisan officer, a young woman with gray hair and a face turned prematurely haggard by everything she's seen. After a few moments, Dafni realizes he knows her. They grew up in the same part of Zagreb. Her partisan comrades don't know she's a Jew.

When she discovers the identity of the two parachutists, their hearts open, and the three of them talk into the night. The partisan tells them of her suffering and that of the Jews of this part of Europe. The parachutists, for their part, tell her of the young people in Zion, and "bring her news of the land being built." When Dafni recounts this story, the Hebrew word that he uses for "news," *besora*, is also the word for "gospel."

ON JUNE 20, two weeks after Hannah disappears on the border between Yugoslavia and Hungary, headquarters receives information that she has successfully reached Budapest as planned. Just under a month later, from Yugoslavia, Dafni reports the same, adding that the Frenchman accompanying her was killed at the border. Some of these reports may simply have been garbled, or the kind of rumor passed on by agents hoping to be paid for giving customers what they want to hear. Or they could be disinformation from the Dogwood double agents who work for the Mossad while serving the Abwehr: The Germans would want to convince Hannah's handlers that she's operational, because if they have her radio they can start transmitting in her name.

Months pass. By early fall, several sources are reporting that Hannah really is in Budapest. But not as planned—as an inmate at the dreaded military prison Margit Körút.

A report in the files identifies this facility as "the worst in Hungary," housing the regime's military court and interrogation chambers. It's also the site of executions by firing squad. Hannah is in the custody of the Hungarian gendarmerie under Gestapo control. The gendarmes, a former prisoner tells Hannah's handlers, have "always excelled at cruelty and always had an overt spirit of anti-Semitism."

Soon the news is much worse. "We very much regret to inform you," Simonds writes to his Mossad counterparts in October, "that we have received a report that Miss Hannah Senesh was captured and shot by the Germans whilst carrying out a mission in enemy-occupied territory."

By the end of the same month, this information has reached the Zionist leader himself, Ben-Gurion. Along with the report of Hannah's execution he's given a copy of "Happy Is the Match," which has traveled from the Yugoslav forest all the way to Tel Aviv. He copies the poem solemnly into his journal. The match has flared.

But this information is wrong. Hannah is alive.

8

PRISON

In 1988 the producer and director Menahem Golan (*The Delta Force*, *Superman IV*, *Operation Thunderbolt*) released the Hollywood production *Hanna's War*. It was the same year as *Rain Man* and *Big*. The reviews were unkind and the box office even worse, which must have been especially disappointing for the producer, who was born in Mandatory Palestine in 1929, and was fifteen when the parachutists were sent into Europe. For Golan the movie was a passion project, an attempt to tell a story dear to him in his own art form, which happened to be mid-budget American action films. The film did enjoy a modest life as a staple of Jewish history classes.

Some of the plot is concocted melodrama, like the scene where Hannah, with her British uniform and submachine gun, joins a stirring attack by partisan cavalry against a Nazi weapons train, only to find it full of Jews going to a death camp. This never happened. But anyone who scoffs at the script must acknowledge that what the least believable plot twists have in common is that they're true.

The scene, for example, where Hannah's brother, Gyuri, who's been trapped in Europe and whom she hasn't seen for five years, arrives in Palestine by sea precisely on the day she leaves for the mission. What are the odds of that? They manage a brief meeting, their first as adults, and their last. A photographer snaps a photo of them, George smiling at the camera, sharp in his European suit, Hannah in her RAF tunic, beaming sideways at her brother as a car passes behind them in the street.

Or the part where she's dropped to infiltrate Hungary precisely as the Germans seal the border, dashing her plans and reducing her to frantic tears. This is actually what happened, as I've recounted.

But the final acts are the ones that truly stretch the limits of credibility.

TWO WOMEN BEGIN their day in a quiet house in Budapest. It's before 8 a.m., June 17, 1944.

Upstairs, still in bed, is Margit Dajka, star of stage and screen. Downstairs, moving in her housecoat among heavy couches and tables, is the playwright's widow. The actress, a paying boarder, is posing as the owner of the house. Her old friend the widow, who is the real owner, poses as the tenant. Were Béla still alive, writing at a desk in the study, the theatrical premise would be obvious to him. A reader may be skeptical that this really happened. But whatever the talents of her late husband, the widow Katherine is known for

PRISON

elegance and stoicism, but never for invention. This description is from her written account.

An unfamiliar man comes up the street, examining a slip of paper. He pauses by the iron gate.

Katherine opens the door. She knows she lives in a time of terror and arbitrary arrest. Outside the capital, the Germans and their Hungarian collaborators are killing the Jews of provincial Hungary. Nearly nothing will be left of them. The Jews in the city limits of Budapest have been left for last, subjected in the meantime to immiseration. They scramble for foreign papers and safe houses. Katherine's connections and money have spared her the worst of it so far. Her friend the actress is Christian, and their role reversal is an attempt to keep the home from being seized as Jewish property. Katherine doesn't always wear the yellow star because she's heard of a clause exempting Jews who can claim cultural achievements, and she has been citing "the literary activities of my late husband."

The man wears civilian clothes, but he's a policeman. He's looking for a Mrs. Béla Szegő.

There's no one here of that name, Katherine replies, in her account of this morning. She's telling the truth. For a moment it's possible to hope that what's coming might still be averted. A simple error: The policeman has the wrong house.

HE CHECKS HIS SLIP again and corrects the family name. She lets him in.

The policeman doesn't know much, just that she's wanted at military headquarters. She must come with him.

The actress gets out of bed and rushes downstairs to entertain the policeman while Katherine gets dressed. The officer is someone who takes an interest in theater and film. He remains polite in the presence of these refined women, even if one is a Jew.

At the headquarters on Horthy Miklos Boulevard, Katherine is turned over to a tall Hungarian in civilian dress but of military bearing: the interrogator Rósza. He leads her to his office and motions toward a chair.

In the Hollywood film this Rósza is played as a sadist, a sweating pervert—it's overdone, even if he really was a torturer. In Katherine's description of the meeting, he seems cruel but controlled.

The interrogator installs himself behind a desk and observes her. Katherine still cannot fathom what he wants. She's startled when he asks about her daughter.

Why, Rósza wants to know, did Hannah leave home? What has she been doing in the years since she emigrated? How often does she write?

Katherine tells the truth, or what she thinks is the truth: Hannah left before the war and now lives at an agricultural commune on the Mediterranean coast in Palestine. She hasn't seen her daughter for nearly five years, and the fact of Hannah's safety is one of the few consolations she has left. She's being honest. She knows nothing more.

When the interrogator seems satisfied, he has her sign a typed statement.

"Now then," he says, in Katherine's account. "Where do you really think your daughter is now—this minute?"

PRISON

She repeats the same answer: Palestine.

No, Rósza says.

Behind Katherine, the door opens.

SHE TURNS.

Four men lead in a woman with matted hair and two black eyes. Katherine doesn't recognize her at first. Red welts mark the prisoner's neck and cheeks, and one of her front teeth is missing.

Katherine clutches the edge of the desk with both hands as the floor seems to drop away.

"Mother," cries the stranger, "forgive me."

ON THE BORDER eight days earlier, after the scene in the forest with the folded paper, Hannah crosses.

She's with Tissandier, the escaped French POW working for British intelligence, whose testimony survives. With them are the two Hungarian Jews, Peter Kolusz and Sandor Fleischman, who are going back to help more refugees escape. After their travails crossing the two rivers at the frontier, the four finally reach the far side in daylight.

They take their first steps on Hungarian soil, walking through a wheat field until they see a road. They stop to put the final touches on their civilian disguises.

A peasant is working nearby. Peter and Sandor go over to ask the name of the nearby hamlet, then walk toward the homes to look for a smuggler they're meant to contact. Hannah and Tissandier stay concealed by the road.

There are gendarmes around, Hungarian policemen with cock's feathers in their hats. They seem unusually alert. Maybe the authorities have been tipped off by the couriers who, as we now know, work for the Germans. Maybe this is just the normal nervousness of a wartime border.

In the village, Peter and Sandor find the smuggler's home, but he's not there. It's now that their clothes, wet and muddy from the river crossing, attract the attention of passing gendarmes, who demand papers. The papers are false. The gendarmes don't notice but are suspicious enough to order the two strangers to come to the police station. Peter panics.

He pulls a pistol from his pocket. Before his comrade Sandor understands what's happening, Peter presses the gun to his own head and pulls the trigger. He crumples on the road and chaos erupts around them.

Hiding in the brush some distance away, Hannah and Tissandier don't know what's happening, but they see the area come alive with troops running and shouting orders. They flatten themselves and pray not to be seen, but when they lift their heads they find themselves facing twenty muzzles.

The gendarmes search their belongings and the vicinity. It doesn't take them long to find the radio. When they do, one of the gendarmes raises his rifle butt and smashes in the Frenchman's teeth.

PRISON

. . .

At the fortress at Csáktornya they're "questioned," but Tissandier doesn't remember many questions being asked. He has a sharp eye for detail, and his account needs no help from me.

> *There, before questioning us at all, they tied our feet and our hands together, and three men took it in turn and beat the soles of our feet. Then they made me walk with my bruised feet along a gnarled trunk, which was hideously painful. Afterward I received 50 strokes [on] the hands with a stick. Then I was made to lie on my face, and at the slightest move I received a blow on the back. Finally I was made to run round the cellar and the passage. At each corner I got a blow from the stick. There were four of the brutes, two of whom would be easily recognizable again. One of them was a man of about 172–74 centimeters in height, very powerfully built, with a square face, and hard but fairly intelligent expression. The other was smaller—about 168 centimeters—very dark and exceptionally ugly, with a typical torturer's head.*

When the session is over, the three prisoners are handed back to the regular gendarmes, who drag them into a cell by their hair and manacle their wrists and feet. They're told to look at a certain point high on the wall of the cell, and if their gaze drops, they get the rifle butt. Tissandier and Sandor receive the worst of it. The actual interrogations begin only at their next stop, Szombathely, which is where the torturers start in on Hannah.

OUT OF THE SKY

The Frenchman doesn't know what happens to her in the chamber, but it seems to be here that one of her front teeth is knocked or pulled out. She confesses that the radio is hers.

HANNAH HAS BEEN in the interrogation room for hours, her feet whipped, her body beaten with rubber truncheons, no part of her left unbruised, when she finally reveals her real name. The interrogator Rósza is surprised. The name isn't common. "Are you related in some way to the writer Béla Senesh?" he asks.

This scene is fiction—it appears in a 1969 young adult book familiar to a generation of Israelis, *The Parachutist Who Never Came Back*. It's part of the story that many remember. Not true, that is, but truly part of the myth.

"He was my father," the prisoner says with pride. Rósza pauses the torture session.

"EARLIER, THERE WAS QUITE AN EVENT—for 60 fillér, I discovered my future." This is Hannah, writing in Budapest in July 1938, before her seventeenth birthday. There's just over a year to go before the war begins.

"A gypsy girl told my fortune by reading my left palm. Needless to say, it was vague and frivolous. She said I'll be engaged at 18, and my husband will have a car. Then she said that he won't be rich, but we'll live very happily together. I'll have one son."

The girl said Hannah had been in love twice—which is possible, she writes, but "neither of them was really love"—and had a suitor, which is nonsense. "Then she said someone abroad is thinking of me (now that's definitely not true). She also said I'll receive a letter soon that will make me happy—well, we'll see about that.

"I wrote it all down so I can check back on it later. The gypsy girl had beautiful eyes."

Six years after the encounter with the fortune teller, Hannah turns twenty-three in prison. After making her way from Budapest to the Land of Israel and then to Cairo, and from there to Bari, then by airdrop into Yugoslavia and across the border to Hungary, she's now a short tram ride from where she was born.

IN A BATTERED SUITCASE stored at Hannah's kibbutz, a world away from the prison, as yet unread by anyone else, is a sheet of paper with another poem. It's just thirteen words in careful Hebrew, one of them misspelled. Her kibbutz is on the beach near the Roman aqueduct at Caesarea, and this is where the poem was composed. The lines capture a moment of contemplation on the sand.

> *My Lord—may these things never end*
> *The sand and the sea*
> *The murmur of water*
> *The lightning in the sky*
> *A human prayer.*

The word "human"—in Hebrew, *adam*, as in the name of the first human—seems to have been one of Hannah's favorites and recurs in her writing. In the handwritten original of this poem, in the word *le'olam*, "never," she substitutes the letter *aleph* for the similar-sounding *ayin*. It's a common slip for a new Hebrew speaker, but for anyone raised on what is probably the most famous song in modern Hebrew, encountering the error is as jarring as finding a spelling mistake in Yeats. It reminds a reader that Hannah spoke Hebrew for only a few years, and that she came from somewhere else.

When the poem is discovered, in 1945, the words are put to music by a gifted composer, David Zehavi, a worker from another kibbutz. Zehavi says afterward that when he was handed the paper the melody came to him in minutes, after which he didn't change a note. Hannah called her poem "A Walk to Caesarea." But the song is better known by the repetition of the first word of her Hebrew text, which the composer added to suit the tune. "Eli Eli" is performed so often that it has been flattened into kitsch, like its author, making it hard to hear what a beautiful song it really is, or to appreciate the seamless marriage of the melody and the words. There are countless covers, not only from Israel. While writing this book amid the Russian invasion of Ukraine, I was surprised to encounter a video of a poignant new version sung by burly Slavic men in camouflage—a Ukrainian military choir.

HANNAH SPENDS HOURS pacing her cell. Using a pencil and some cheap paper, she writes a few lines. They're no longer in Hebrew. She has returned to her mother tongue.

> *One, two, three . . . eight is the length.*
> *Two paces are the width.*

PRISON

Life flutters as a question mark.
One, two three . . . maybe in a week.
Or the end of the moon will find me still here.
But death hovers over my head.
I would have turned 23 this July.
I gambled on a number in a game of chance.
The dice spun. I lost.

Today this paper is kept in a gallery of literary treasures at Israel's National Library, displayed with the work of writers like David Grossman and the songstress Naomi Shemer. Also nearby is the suicide note of Stefan Zweig from 1942. Hannah's reading list shows that she read Zweig, who, like her, managed to escape the Nazis. He made it from his native Austria to safety in Brazil, but he and his wife killed themselves anyway, "the world of my own language having disappeared for me, and my spiritual home, Europe, having destroyed itself."

IF YOU LOOK FOR the Margit Körút prison now, you'll find a park full of students and mothers with strollers, next to a mall with a Benetton. The building was demolished by the communist totalitarians who followed the fascists in this city. Opposite the mall, across tracks where yellow trams whir back and forth, is a bronze bust of a young woman wearing an old-fashioned pilot's cowl and aviator goggles, looking valiantly at the sky. The statue is new but the style vaguely Soviet. It's Hannah. Under her name on the plinth is the word *költő*—poet.

OUT OF THE SKY

In 1944 this place is the architectural embodiment of terror. Inside the prison are interrogation chambers and cells arrayed around a central courtyard, where prisoners are sometimes allowed a few minutes of sunlight and sometimes shot.

HANNAH ISN'T THE ONLY parachutist here.

In another cell is Joel Palgi, who crossed into Hungary shortly after her. This is his Hebrew name; his birth name, which I mention because it will shortly be relevant, is Emil Nussbacher. With Joel is his partner, Peretz, born with the name Franz Goldstein. After setting out on their mission, the pair didn't last long. The Gestapo knew where they were. In fact, Hitler himself had an eye on them.

This hardly seems credible. Our parachutists are players in a marginal operation in a world war. Certainly the Führer has enough to contend with as his fronts crumble in the east and west in the summer of 1944. And yet the documents leave no doubt. In a compendium of German papers related to the extermination of Hungary's Jews, I find an exchange of letters between Nazi officials in Budapest and Berlin under the heading, "Telegram from ALTENBURG to VEESENMAYER Transmitting HITLER's Orders with Respect to the Palestinian Parachutists Captured in Hungary."

On July 8, Veesenmayer, the SS man serving as Hitler's direct representative in Hungary, notifies Berlin of the arrest of British parachutists sent from Italy. Some of the details seem garbled—the Hungarian gendarmes say they found nine parachutes, but the number of captured parachutists is given as four, along with two

PRISON

transmitters. Four is the number in Hannah's party. But as the arrest is reported to have occurred in early July, and Hannah crossed several weeks earlier, this may refer to a different British mission. Frontier guards also arrested "bandits," the report continues, who were sent into Hungary to "transport Hungarian refugees and fleeing prisoners" into Yugoslavia. This sounds like what Peter and Sandor, the two Hungarians who infiltrated with Hannah, were trying to do.

The SS report mentions two British agents, Emil Nussbacher and Franz Goldstein, by name, identifying them as Hungarian Jews and current citizens of British Palestine. The pair made it to Budapest, where "they were under observation the entire time." Both men "were members of the Zionist youth movement, moved to Palestine in 1939, received Palestinian citizenship, and later voluntarily joined the British army." The first is a lieutenant, the second an enlisted radioman. They were dropped in April, according to the Nazi report, received by the partisans, and crossed into Hungary in June. All of this is accurate.

The report is sent to Berlin. There it reaches Ribbentrop, the Reich foreign minister. And from the hands of this minister, the paper goes to Hitler himself.

A senior aide in the foreign ministry, Altenburg, wires the Nazi envoy in Budapest on July 12. The heading is "Top Secret/Classified." The Führer has seen the report, writes the aide, and has added a personal note. Three words appear on the page in Hitler's handwriting. "*Sind zu ershciessen!*"

"They should be shot!"

OUT OF THE SKY

. . .

JOEL'S MEMOIR, *A Great Wind Cometh*, a bestseller in Hebrew after the war, includes an account of Hannah's meeting with her mother in the office of the interrogator Rósza. According to Joel, he heard the story from Hannah in prison.

Under torture, Hannah has already revealed her real name and mission, but not what the interrogator wants more than anything—the radio code, which would allow the Nazis to transmit to her British handlers under her identity, feeding them disinformation and entrapping other agents.

When she speaks to Joel, Hannah describes seeing her mother for the first time in the interrogator's room: "I don't remember what I said, or what she said to me. I uttered words and syllables without any meaning, like a baby who doesn't know how to talk."

"Aniko," her mother says, recovering from the shock and speaking her childhood nickname—and it's at this moment that Hannah understands what she has done. She is a person with words for almost everything, in more than one language, but now she has none. The moment is unspeakable.

After Katherine is led away, the interrogator addresses the prisoner in a friendly tone. "I'm sorry I resorted to extreme methods with you," he says. "After all, you are the daughter of the great writer Béla Senesh." But if she doesn't reveal everything she knows, he tells her, he'll have her mother killed.

"No," Hannah shouts, "no, don't touch Mother. You don't have the right."

"I'll have her executed as you watch," says the interrogator.

PRISON

"Kill me, torture me, tear my flesh, just don't touch my mother," Hannah screams.

"The code," says Rósza.

"Mercy, Mother, mercy," begs Hannah.

"The code..."

No sooner has Katherine left her daughter than she is arrested herself.

Her captors are both Hungarians and Germans, including one Nazi she describes as a gaunt man with a Death's Head badge on his cap, a member of the Totenkopf SS. Before she's sent into the prison as an inmate, they demand her money and jewelry. When she hesitates too long, the SS man, whose face she thinks resembles his skull insignia, slaps her so hard she spins around. She is so dazed by the day's events, Katherine records of this moment, that she doesn't feel the blow—"as if a stranger had taken my place, or a mechanized puppet."

Two uniformed women search her body and escort her to a cell. When the door swings open, she sees a room that reminds her of a hospital ward, with six beds. The inmates sitting on the beds turn their heads toward the new arrival.

It's a cell that seems to be reserved for women of the upper class. She recognizes one prisoner as the divorced wife of Baron Lajos Hatvany and later finds that the others include the wife of a Jewish member of parliament, denounced by her butler for anti-Nazi sentiments, as well as the widow Héderváry, whose husband is accused of collaboration with the Allies. The women pass the time playing bridge with cards improvised from scraps of paper. There's an argument over who will clean the toilet: They're supposed to take turns, but one inmate, Countess Zichy, claims she's incapable of such a task. It's left to Baroness Hatvany, of all people, to insist that no one is exempt and to demonstrate the use of the brush and scrubbing powder.

The inmates' squabbles are of no interest to Katherine, who can think only about whether Hannah is still alive. She knows enough of her daughter's personality, and of the men holding her, to fear the answer is no. Hannah won't give them what they want, and they'll show no mercy. The following night, when her cellmates are asleep, she finds a razor blade among their toiletries and slashes her wrist.

ELSEWHERE IN BUDAPEST a famous scandal is unfolding. The setting is the office of Rezső Kasztner, journalist and lawyer, head of the Jewish relief committee in Budapest, and a Zionist official with ties to the Labor movement leadership in Tel Aviv. Today he's remembered mainly as the central figure in the Kasztner Affair, which plays out precisely as the parachutists' mission unravels. The two stories have been filed in very different historical categories, both oversimplified—one "collaboration," the other "heroism"—but they intersect.

Possessed of considerable charm and political talents, Kasztner has become a go-between with the murderous Nazi bureaucrat Eichmann and his henchmen. In one of the war's strangest episodes, Kasztner is trying to strike a deal to buy the lives of Jews from the Nazis with money and Allied war matériel, including thousands of trucks. The Zionist movement is desperate to save whoever can be

PRISON

saved and will try anything. The deal, known as Blood for Goods, doesn't happen, and could never happen. The Allies aren't about to arm the enemy just to save Jews. But the talks allow Kasztner to get his Nazi contacts to approve a goodwill gesture: a single shipment of people of his own choosing who'll be spared death and allowed to reach Switzerland. This is the famous or infamous Kasztner train, with 1,684 people on board.

The furor surrounding Kasztner begins then, in the summer of 1944, and never really ends. "After all the reading, listening, and searching, I feel I have discovered the real Rezső Kasztner—an extraordinary man who played a high-stakes game of roulette with the devil. And won," writes Anna Porter in her 2007 book *Kasztner's Train*. No Jew in the Holocaust saved more Jews than Kasztner did, even if he didn't jump out of a plane or hold a gun and instead practiced skills of a more slippery and ignoble kind.

The 2016 book *Kasztner's Crime*, by Paul Bogdanor, portrays the same man not just as a Nazi dupe but as a traitor. Kasztner eats and drinks with Nazis, enjoys the special treatment, knows what awaits the rest of Hungary's doomed Jews but decides not to tell them. Sounding a warning, and perhaps sparking revolt among the condemned, would endanger him, his friends and relatives, and the other prominent people on his passenger list. In this version, the famous train is not a victory struck by Kasztner against the Nazis—it's the price he's paid for his collaboration in the murder of everyone else. At the Nuremberg tribunal after the war, when there's no conceivable reason to humor Nazis any longer, Kasztner takes the unimaginable step of offering character witness for the SS criminal Kurt Becher, one of his contacts in Budapest. His testimony helps

Becher evade certain execution and enjoy a long, undeserved life as a respectable German businessman.

The war is barely over when Kasztner is first accused of collaboration, but it doesn't stick. By the early 1950s he's living in Israel, working as a newspaper editor and a minor government official. Because he's close to the Labor party then in power, the party of Ben-Gurion, accusing Kasztner becomes a way for the Israeli right to attack the left for failing to save the Jews of Europe. This is a familiar form of storytelling in Jewish history. The Jews are always outnumbered and beset by greater powers, whether the Babylonians, Assyrians, Christians, Nazis, or clerics of fundamentalist Islam, and regularly blame each other for problems beyond their control. It's not a rational analysis but it's very old—the same phenomenon can be glimpsed among the Jewish factions inside Jerusalem during the Roman siege of 70 CE—and is a feature of a small people under immense pressure, desperate to believe in their own agency.

In 1955, Kasztner's allies in the Israeli government file an unwise libel suit against one of his detractors, a gadfly from Jerusalem who called him a collaborator in a mimeographed broadsheet. Kasztner takes the stand confident, but then sees his story disintegrate under examination by his opponent's talented lawyer. One of this lawyer's moves is to conjure up the image of Hannah Senesh, doing so through the testimony of her mother, Katherine. The court is meant to grasp that Hannah, who is in Budapest at the same time, is the image of a true hero—brave, pure of heart, and unavailable to testify. Kasztner, on the other hand, with his deals and lies, is a traitor, even if he did save 1,684 people and she saved none.

PRISON

The trial ends with a shocking decision against Kasztner. The judge rules that the charge of collaboration is accurate, that he "sold his soul to the devil"—a phrase that adheres to Rezső Kasztner permanently and remains, to this day, what the average Israeli knows about him. The verdict is later overturned on appeal, but by this time Kasztner has been assassinated by vigilantes in Tel Aviv.

THIS SHADOWY BUSINESS is playing out in Budapest precisely as Hannah crosses the border on June 9, 1944, followed ten days later by Joel and Peretz.

According to the plan they hatched in Yugoslavia before their infiltration, the three parachutists will meet after Sunday prayers at St. Stephen's Basilica, home to the mummified hand of the Magyar king of that name. The two men make it and wait outside the church. But Hannah never shows up.

Alone and frightened in this city where Nazis and collaborators seem to lurk in every stairwell and passage, Joel and Peretz decide to contact a local figure they think will help them—the Jewish official Kasztner. But they are misinformed. When they show up at his office unannounced and reveal who they are, he's angry. The appearance of these British agents will complicate his delicate talks with the Nazis and could upend his deal. At this very moment, the passengers selected for life on his rescue train are housed at an empty Jewish school on the outskirts of town, awaiting their departure. He isn't going to jeopardize their lives for these two.

The Nazis, Kasztner tells the two parachutists, already know they're in Budapest. They are aghast, but of course it's true. The

Nazi dispatch from Budapest to Berlin says that after crossing the border, Joel and Peretz "were under observation the entire time." Both end up arrested by the Gestapo.

At the famous trial in Israel a decade later, Joel is called to testify on Kasztner's behalf. By this time, Joel is known as a war hero and as the author of a famous account of the mission. His book is oddly kind to Kasztner, even though the man played a role in Joel's arrest, and even though Joel's own parents and sister had been left off Kasztner's list and murdered in a death camp. Kasztner is close to the men running the new state of Israel, who see him as one of their own and view his train as a rare rescue operation that succeeded. Joel is an idealist, a loyal soldier of the Zionist movement. He agrees to testify to Kasztner's innocence, presumably because he's told that's what the country needs him to do.

But under cross-examination he stumbles. The skilled lawyer opposing Kasztner picks apart not just Joel's testimony but the veracity of his memoir. In fact the very idea of historical literature is dissected on the stand. The author is forced to admit that he manipulated facts in *A Great Wind Cometh*, that the real Kasztner is a darker figure than the one described in its pages. Joel claims the book is nonfiction. It has been marketed as a true account. But faced with contradictions in the text, the humiliated author concedes that it's "a novel, not history."

Joel's publisher cancels the next edition of the book and apologizes to the public for the "deception." It's only twenty years later that Joel publishes a new version with assurances that this one is true. The new edition contains a more negative portrait of Kasztner, though it's still ambiguous, to the author's credit. Kasztner was a man faced with impossible choices. Joel dies shortly after publication, in 1978. He ends the book with the following thought:

> *The rule still holds:*
> *If you go and don't return—you'll be a hero.*
> *If you go and do return—you'll be judged.*
> *If you do nothing—you'll sit in judgment of others.*
> *But a nation will survive as long as there are those who say:*
> *If I don't go, who will?*

WHILE UNDER INTERROGATION in Gestapo custody, Joel remembers a scene from earlier that year. He's still in MI9 training in Cairo, sitting in a luxurious leather armchair in a room overlooking Soliman Pasha Square, studying maps with Hannah while Enzo tries to make them laugh by quoting excerpts from P. G. Wodehouse. Hannah looks up from her map of Yugoslavia. What happens, she asks suddenly, if they're caught with their transmitters?

The two men look at her. It seems that no one has yet dared to explicitly raise this possibility. Enzo raises a finger, his mannerism before imparting significant advice. Each of them, he says, must carry poison.

The two parachutists, who are in their early twenties, consider the possibility of suicide. They're thinking of themselves—this is before anyone knows that the older man is planning to jump too. Enzo peers at them through his round spectacles. "They'll torture you," he says. "And you should know: No hero can withstand torture." There will be no mercy, even for Hannah.

Joel describes an awful silence and a feeling of "fingers of cold steel gripping my throat." He leaps from the armchair. Enzo has no right to say such things, he shouts, and storms in fury from the room. They ignore Enzo's advice. That summer Joel finds himself nearly broken by torture, without cyanide or any other way to end it. He considers slamming his head against the iron leg of the bed in his cell, but he can't summon the strength. It's then, he writes, that he finds a little metal rectangle wedged into the bed frame—a US Army dog tag, a relic from a previous occupant by the name of Robert Johnson. Joel wonders how the American reached this cell and what became of him. He bends the tag back and forth until it snaps in the middle, then uses the sharp edge to cut the vein in his wrist. After he blacks out, he hallucinates refugee ships and his missing parents. He feels himself falling through the air with a chute that won't open. He wakes in the shower with a guard dousing him with cold water, a rough tourniquet on his arm. They won't let him die.

Guards at the Margit Körút prison take evening roll call, shouting out names in the corridor. He freezes upon hearing one that he knows.

A woman's voice comes from another cell: *Ja*. Hannah is here.

KATHERINE'S SUICIDE is foiled by her cellmate the baroness, who turns out not to be asleep. She runs over and binds Katherine's arm with two handkerchiefs, scolding her furiously—this reckless act could get them all punished. Within a day or two, the baroness is taken from the cell anyway and deported with the wife of the Jewish parliamentarian. At this time Katherine still doesn't know what "deported" means. She hears about the extermination camps only later that summer, when the cellmates are joined by a Polish woman who's been wandering the roads of Europe for years, and who constantly tells the others that their only future is Auschwitz. Katherine has never heard that name.

The same morning the baroness disappears, Katherine is summoned for further interrogation. She's following a guard down a flight of stairs when she passes a young inmate scrubbing the floor. This prisoner seems to know her story, and she whispers that Hannah is here.

One evening not long afterward, the key turns in the door of Katherine's cell. When it swings open, she sees the prisoner Hilda, whose beauty and German parentage have won her privileges from the guards. These include occasional responsibility for the ring of keys that unlock the cells—a strange security lapse that must be part of fraying discipline in the prison as the Nazis grow weaker in the summer of 1944, and as Hungary's loyalties become uncertain.

Hilda tells Katherine to climb to the window of the cell and look out, even though this is forbidden. Across the prison yard, at another window on the same floor, she sees her daughter. Hannah waves.

The beautiful inmate comes another evening, and this time she beckons Katherine out of the cell and leads her to a nearby toilet. When the door opens, Hannah is there.

Hannah smiles sadly, looking almost like herself again. The welts have faded and her hair is combed, but the gap in her front teeth makes it impossible to forget what's been done to her. Hannah says she lost the tooth in parachute training, but her mother knows she's lying. "If all I lose in this venture is a tooth, we can both be grateful," Hannah says.

As for how she ended up here, Hannah will say only that she's a "radio officer" in the British army, that she volunteered for a mission she couldn't complete. Hilda knocks on the bathroom door. Their time is up.

THE RUMBLE OF ARTILLERY grows in volume by the week as the Red Army advances toward Budapest. The prison guards become friendlier. In early summer twenty women had crowded into Katherine's six-bed cell, but by the end of August conditions have improved so much that she has her own cot.

On one night that is exceptionally still, Katherine can't sleep. She feels certain that Hannah is awake too. She creeps past her sleeping cellmates and looks out the window, the moon so bright that the prison yard almost seems bathed in daylight. The wall opposite Katherine is illuminated, her own side of the yard in shadow. "I clearly saw Hannah silhouetted against the half-open window, wearing her light-blue dressing gown, her hair softly framing her lovely face." Her daughter isn't looking at her. The moonlight glows around her head like a "soft halo."

Does Hannah really have a light-blue dressing gown in prison? The scene certainly expresses the black truth of the moment—a mother trapped in a malevolent maze, imprisoned with her own daughter, whom she can see but not touch, who is in deadly danger but whom she can't save.

PRISON

. . .

KATHERINE IS MOVED from the prison to a less brutal facility on the outskirts of the city, then finally told she can go home. It's late September, and the Soviets are closing in. Liberation seems imminent.

She spends the next few weeks—her first as a free woman and the last before the city's final descent into homicidal and suicidal delusion—in a frantic round of government offices and law firms, trying to get help for her daughter. Hannah has also asked her to find a Hebrew Bible, and she tries, but all the Jewish shops have been shuttered, and even a store specializing in religious books in Deák Square is surprised at her request. They have the Bible in every language, it seems, except the one in which it was written.

She asks for help from Kasztner, who's known to have the ear of the authorities, but he won't even meet her. She finally finds a lawyer, a Dr. Szelecsényi, who is willing to take the case. He's Christian—Jews can no longer practice. The lawyer manages to meet Hannah at the prison and studies the details of her arrest. She will certainly be convicted of espionage, he informs Katherine. The sentence will be long. But this won't matter, he believes, because the war is nearly over.

THE LAWYER'S MEETING with Hannah is on October 14. The next day is when Horthy announces the end of the war and is then deposed, imprisoned, and replaced by the overtly Nazi regime of the Arrow Cross.

Inside the prison on the day of the fascist coup, the inmates hear gunfire outside and struggle to understand what it means. One of them hears a guard say something about bridges being captured—but by whom? Some think it's the Red Army vanguard.

Now they hear tanks rumbling through the streets. But oddly, the tanks aren't firing, and no one is firing at them. They can't be Russian. From his cell, Joel hears one of the guards shout that the captain in No. 28 has been released, and that's when he understands. This captain is a Nazi sympathizer who'd just been arrested when it looked like Hungary was about to surrender. If he's going free, the fascists are in charge.

Arrow Cross loyalists now take over the prison, and the days of laxity end with a spate of executions in the yard. From the cells, the prisoners hear the tramp of boots when the firing squad marches in, a few last words shouted by the condemned, the call "Aim!" and the volley. Joel counts a dozen executions in the space of two days. It's around this time that the mistaken reports of Hannah's death reach MI9.

In the streets outside, Jews are seized by roving gangs of Hungarian men and marched to the banks of the Danube. The murderers line them up and tie them together with wire, then shoot only a few of them. This saves ammunition and is better sport: All the victims fall into the river, and those who aren't shot will drown. The grandfather of a friend of mine, a former army officer named for the old Austro-Hungarian emperor Franz Joseph, is one of thousands whose lives end this way. The bodies float for a while before the river removes the evidence and the next group is marched to the bank.

In the prison, a fragile order still prevails. If Hannah were outside on the street, she might simply be shot into the river. But here, as a captured traitor and spy, her fate will be decided by military tribunal.

No official records of the proceedings have ever surfaced. In their absence, the most important account is the one in Joel's memoir. His version is based on what he heard from others who were in the courtroom and shared his cell—the Frenchman Tissandier and Sandor, the Hungarian, who were captured with Hannah and tried at the same time. The only official document I've seen is a strange one, issued after the collapse of communist Hungary nearly fifty years later, declaring the verdict void.

In the movie the trial is the great climax. Hannah is brought into court with her hair coiffed, in a striking white blouse. The director lacks the courage to have Maruschka Detmers play the heroine with a missing front tooth. Hannah stands before the court and gives a defiant speech in which she indicts the judges. It is they who are truly on trial! She shames them with her youth and beauty, with the obvious truth of her words.

This is the scene as pictured by someone who admired her but never knew her, based on an account from someone who knew her but wasn't present. Anyone who has read Hannah's writing knows how remarkable her own words would be. All the strands of her old life and her new life, her literary life and her real life, are converging in this room. But we can't hear her voice. There is no point in the story where its absence is more keenly felt.

OUT OF THE SKY

. . .

Hannah looks up at the dais of the military court, at the men about to try her. This is the account published in 1969 for young Israeli readers, *The Parachutist Who Never Came Back*. For a moment, the scene strikes her as a theatrical production in which she's the audience, not the main character.

"Her glance passed over their sealed faces, met their blank eyes. These aren't judges, just bad actors in a poor play, trying to follow the director's instructions." She knows they'll never forgive her for their own misdeeds.

The charge is treason. The sentence will be death. Does she plead guilty?

"No," she says. This is the account from Joel's memoir.

Hannah rises to her feet, her voice clear. "I do not admit to betraying the motherland. I came here on a mission for my own country, my only homeland." She was raised to love the language and art of the country of her birth, to believe that the suffering of its people would open their hearts to the plight of others. "My father was a writer," she tells the court, "and he instilled in me the belief that good will vanquish evil in the end."

But when she grew up, she tells them, she realized she had no place in Hungary. She saw the laws against Jews, the humiliation of people who believed they were equal citizens. She witnessed their separation and isolation, and finally their murder. She didn't betray her country, she says, because this isn't her country. She has come from her real country to save the Jews from people who've betrayed the vision she was taught.

"The traitors are those who brought disaster on the nation," she concludes in this account, which is the best we have. The appeal to literature certainly sounds like Hannah.

KATHERINE GETS INTO THE CORRIDOR, close enough to see a sign on the door reading, "Anna Senesh and accomplices." But military trials are closed to the public, so she can't get in, and must wait outside the building. She may be a free woman, but she's risking her life—armed fascists are hunting Jews in the street. There's a crowd waiting with her, presumably relatives of other inmates whose fates hang in the balance inside.

When the hearing ends before noon Hannah is led out and sees her mother. The guards allow them a moment. "I was shaken to my core," Katherine records. "But she was excited and flushed, her eyes confident." Hannah is led away through the crowd to be returned to her cell.

The next day is October 29. In the prison, Joel wakes up to new blasts of artillery fire. The windowpanes rattle. The Russians are barely ten miles away. The air raids are now so fierce that Katherine doesn't dare venture outside to the prison. Budapest is being blown to pieces and is consuming itself from within. A week passes.

JOEL AND HIS COMRADE PERETZ are in their cell. They've been running through different plans for escape—removing the window bars, descending to the prison yard on a rope of ripped blankets, killing the guards and climbing the outer wall to the street. This is less a real plan than a way to pass time without losing hope. Within weeks the guards will march them from the cell and load them into boxcars bound for camps deeper into Axis territory. It's then that Joel really will make a remarkable escape, sawing his way out of the boxcar and jumping. With him through the hole goes the Frenchman Tissandier, which is how both survive to tell the story. Peretz, in a different car, is never seen again.

But this morning they're still prisoners, crouching silently on folded blankets, backs to the wall, huddled close to keep warm. A shot rings out. Maybe two—the second may be an echo.

Executions at the prison go according to a script: the stomp of boots, the reading of the sentence loud enough for the whole prison to hear, and only then the shots. They heard no preliminaries this time, so they think it may be an accidental discharge by a guard—maybe one of the new ones, poorly trained old men pressed into service because there's no one else left.

One of the other inmates scrambles up to the window but can't see much. It's about to rain.

THAT MORNING KATHERINE finally braves the streets, going not to the prison but to a military office at the Hadik Barracks to plead for permission to see Hannah. At the barracks she finds everything in chaos, with trucks full of equipment roaring away down the street. A porter tells her there's no point in going into the building—almost everyone has fled. But she insists. The man she needs is Capt. Simon, the military prosecutor in charge of her daughter's case.

When the porter lets her in, she walks the corridors until she finds an office with an open door. Inside, she sees that everything has been packed. There are two clerks, both women in coats and hats, and a single uniformed officer.

Capt. Simon isn't here, the officer tells her. He's at the prison. The officer glances at his watch. "You'd better hurry," he says. She thinks he just means that if she's not quick she'll miss the captain.

She arrives in the prison's forbidding shadow at 10:30 a.m. The premises are oddly quiet, with entire sections that seem deserted. When she finally finds Capt. Simon's office he's not there, but there's a briefcase on the desk by a pair of leather gloves. Their owner must have stepped out to take care of a task, maybe to consult with a colleague. She waits in the hallway until the captain returns, then follows him inside and introduces herself. She'd like a visitor's pass, she says.

"The case no longer has anything to do with me," the captain replies. He seems ill at ease. We don't have an official transcript of this conversation, just as none survives from the trial or the interrogations. Someone seems to have been smart enough to destroy them. It may well have been Capt. Simon himself, who soon disappears into the war-criminal ratlines with his colleague, the interrogator Rósza.

"Since when?" she asks.

"Since yesterday."

An evasive and circular conversation follows. Eventually she asks why there's no date for Hannah's sentencing—or has a sentence already been passed?

"Even if it has been," the captain answers, "I'm not in a position to tell you what it entails."

She repeats the question.

The captain goes to his desk and sits down. He waves her into the chair opposite him.

"Are you a Jew?" he asks. "Or was it only your husband?"

"He was, and I am," she says.

She moves her purse so he can see the yellow star stitched to her coat. The racial hierarchy thus established, this cog in the fascist bureaucracy runs through the story: how Hannah joined the British military and became a radio operator, then flew from Cairo to Italy and from there to Yugoslavia, where she spent time with partisans before infiltrating into Hungary. Her mission was "rescuing Jews and British prisoners of war," the captain explains, crimes against the Hungarian state. She was caught with a transmitter, and her guilt was never in doubt.

Now it must begin to dawn on Katherine where the captain has just been, leaving his briefcase and gloves on his desk.

"Consequently, the military tribunal found her guilty of treason," he continues, "and demanded the supreme penalty. And this... penalty..."

The ellipses are in Katherine's original account. I'm not sure if she means that the captain hesitated, struggling to get the words out, or if the world slowed down for her as it sometimes does at moments of great turbulence, when we seem to be immobilized in a whirlpool.

PRISON

. . .

BY THE END, the prisoner Hannah is forced to regress from the language she acquired to her mother tongue, and from the life she chose to her earlier self, Anna. When she writes her final lines, she has no name at all. She has abandoned poetry and form. The killers are ready in the yard. She seems to have refused both a blindfold and a chance to plead for a pardon.

Her mother is somewhere in the city—she doesn't know how close. Her comrades are oblivious in their cell above the prison yard, about to be startled by the shots. Far to the east is a sunny country, the murmur of water, lightning, another life, but it doesn't matter. She's given a pencil and a sheet of paper that is later found folded in the pocket of her dress.

"Dear Mother, I don't know what to say.

"Only this: A million thanks, and forgive if you can. You know well why words aren't necessary. With endless love, your daughter."

9

HAIM

When the shots are fired in the prison yard in Budapest, Haim the Scythe is in a cold grave one hundred miles due north.

But he's alive. In his hole in the Slovak forest, he knows nothing about Hannah or about the three other parachutists who were with him in the forest camp when the Germans attacked a week before. He won't know for many months. He crouches with David, who escaped with him from the camp. Under the planks that form the crude roof, the two men eat scraps and melt snow on a stove improvised from a can. The temperature drops by the day. They wait, without knowing for what.

To pass the time, Haim tells David about his escape from Europe by sea just before the war, how he was arrested by the British and imprisoned before he came to wear a British uniform himself. David teaches him a Slovak folk song about the bandit Jánošik, the local Robin Hood. When they run out of songs and stories, Haim starts teaching his comrade Hebrew.

Haim awakes one morning with the sense that something has changed. The woods are too quiet. Or maybe it's unusually dark. According to the crude calendar they've been marking with pencil on the planks over their heads, the date is November 14, two weeks after the destruction of their camp.

When Haim tries to move the planks and crawl from the hole, he finds they won't budge. With their shoulders, the two of them push frantically upward. It doesn't help. Snow has fallen all night and they've been buried alive. The planks are bending under the weight pressing down from above, and one has already cracked. "The grave is ready," David says. "All that's left is to die." Haim has been through a great deal and will have to live through more. But in his memoir, this is the most terrifying moment of the war.

They begin to tunnel frantically sideways with a little shovel, with David's pocketknife, and with their freezing fingers. The bunker begins to fill with stones and black earth. Their exertions consume much of the little oxygen that remains, and their breathing becomes strained. They hit an impenetrable tangle of roots. David attacks the roots with his pocketknife, but the blade bends and the roots are impervious. They're trapped.

At this moment, a gun from Act 1 reappears: Haim remembers the saw given to him by the special operations quartermaster in Cairo, the one concealed in a rubber strip and meant for prison bars. He fishes it from the pocket of his fatigues and attacks the roots, which finally begin to splinter and split. After four hours of cutting and digging, by his count, Haim can finally stand but still hasn't reached air. He's upright in a vertical pocket of snow. David passes him the shovel. Now they tunnel upward, building a crude stairway with objects from their bunker—packs, planks, the sleeping bag. Haim's head breaks out of the snow and into the blizzard.

Now he can breathe, but can't see because of the fury of the storm. He wants to make it to a forester's cottage they'd noticed in the trees nearby but can't find it or even remember the right direction. His eyes burn, and he loses feeling in his hands. The cottage isn't far from the grave, but it takes an eternity to crawl there. They burst through the door and slam it shut behind them, then hop around to restore feeling to their limbs. The shack, with a simple room on the ground floor and a little attic beneath the rafters, seems like a palace. It's another day before the storm abates. When he looks out, he sees the Tatra mountains covered in white.

The improved weather brings out the enemy—when the two of them venture outside, they see ski marks near the cabin. So in daytime they hide in the attic, coming down only at night to sleep on the floor. On their tenth day in the cottage they're up in the attic, waiting for nightfall, when the door squeaks.

The two fugitives freeze. They hear footsteps in the little room below them. Then voices speaking Russian.

Haim doesn't know about the fatal error of his comrade Zvi, but he doesn't repeat it. He knows that the Russian language doesn't necessarily mean friends, that it's more likely to mean the same Nazi troops who attacked the camp. "We're lost," he whispers to David. His body begins to shake, and he can't stop. Now the footsteps are ascending the wooden stairs.

From his perch in the attic he first sees a hand holding a German Schmeisser. Then a winter hat, then a face with gray stubble on its cheeks. The two of them raise their hands. "Get up! Come down!" shouts the Russian.

Haim begins to shake even harder, and then to cry—so he tells us in his own admirable account, from a time when weakness of this kind wasn't admired. David helps him stand. "I was ashamed of myself," Haim writes, "but just couldn't push through." He's hungry, and cold, and scared. He's come so far, and he doesn't deserve this ending.

The stubbled soldier takes them downstairs at gunpoint. A second soldier covers them with a rifle while the first goes back up to search the attic.

David's warm hand on his shoulder calms Haim, whose senses begin to return. The second soldier is wearing a Slovak uniform. Slovakia is fascist, but because part of the army has rebelled, the meaning of the uniform is uncertain. This soldier is looking intently at Haim's companion.

"David, don't you recognize me?" the soldier says in a low voice. "We were partisans together in the great uprising." The Russian is still upstairs. The soldier says he's using a Slovak Christian name—his Russian comrade doesn't know he's a Jew, and he wants to keep it that way. The Russians may be fighting with the Allies but they hate Jews too. They should follow his lead, the soldier says, and pretend to be something other than what they are.

So the Russian in the attic is on their side—or at least not on the side most actively trying to kill them. When the soldier comes back downstairs and demands their identities, David claims to be the sole survivor of a rebel Slovak unit, and Haim identifies himself as Lt. Harry Morris, formerly of the British delegation to the rebel forces.

HAIM

The Russian is satisfied. He tells them he's an escaped POW who joined the Slovak rebels and fled Banská Bystrica at the same time they did, in the last days before the Nazis closed in. He's originally a farmer from a kolkhoz in the district of Minsk. They'll join his "unit," which consists of him and six stragglers he's picked up.

These are the first other humans Haim and David have seen in more than three weeks. They celebrate by cooking all of their remaining potatoes and eating until they can't move.

BEFORE LONG the little detachment has joined the bigger partisan formation operating higher in the mountains. The fighters include Slovaks, Red Army soldiers and escaped POWs, a few Ukrainians who have redefected from the collaborators, and a smattering of Hungarians.

The identity of Lt. Harry Morris is a matter of interest to some of the fighters he meets. When he's pressed by a Russian partisan who seems overly curious, he says he's Irish. On one occasion, speaking to a few Red Army paratroopers serving with the partisans, he reveals that he's a Jew from Palestine and immediately regrets it. They tell him that Jews are profiteers and speculators, and refuse to believe he's really a socialist from a farming collective.

As they move through the mountains one day that winter, Haim's platoon comes upon a little cottage in the woods, the peacetime vacation home of some wealthy citizen. They break in. A fighter named Sasha sees a kitchen cupboard with glass windows, releases his safety, and fires a burst at it from the hip—for fun, or out of spite that such a pleasant cottage has the temerity to exist in the same world as the war. The glass shatters, and the partisans trash the rooms, breaking the wooden furniture apart for firewood. A scene comes to Haim from long ago.

He's a schoolboy on winter vacation, in the warm living room of his parents' home. This is before the war, before he escaped Hungary and became a Zionist pioneer, when adventures and tragedies were still only in books. It's late afternoon. In another room his father, the district veterinarian, bends over his papers, preparing a report for the Ministry of Agriculture. His mother comes in with a tray of coffee and bread with butter and honey. At the piano in a third room, his brother attempts Prokofiev. Haim is reading *Siberian Garrison* by Rodion Markovits. A group of Austro-Hungarian officers in a war against Russia have taken over an abandoned mansion with a grand piano. One of them climbs on top, lifts the cover, squats, and takes a shit inside. His comrades laugh.

The young Haim is shocked to read this—so he writes later, in his own book. But now it's he who behaves like a savage, destroying a pretty cottage that someone else built. At this time, he doesn't know if his parents are alive. (His mother is, his father isn't.) His piano-playing brother has escaped to Brazil. The family will never reassemble. He barely remembers what a book is, or classical music. He's alone in a wild forest, beyond civilization. He understands people who shit in grand pianos.

When he meets a Russian officer with access to a radio transmitter, Haim tries to get a message to MI9, scribbling it for the officer in pencil on a piece of paper. He has lost contact with all the others, he writes.

HAIM

I am with the Yegorov unit, 7th Company. Send instructions.
2/Lt Harry Morris

But this message isn't received, if it's ever sent. The others are already dead. His commanders think he is too.

When the Germans try to take a power station in the hills north of Brusno, ascending from the valley with four Tiger tanks, Haim is with the partisans who beat them back. Two fighters are killed, but the number of dead Germans is higher—he counts eleven.

The partisans are still in the snowy forest when the Germans return. Now enemy infantrymen move among the trees in white camouflage smocks. Haim has been put in charge of a few other men and they're hiding in the snow, waiting for the Nazis to come into range, not yet, a few more steps. . . .

When they open fire the Germans spin around in confusion, trying to find their opponents. Haim sees one of them drop. In his account, it's unclear who fires this shot. The question is of interest only because if he did, this would be the first and only German killed by one of the parachutists in the course of the entire mission. But it doesn't seem to be him.

The other Germans crouch and stare into the trees, searching for human shapes or muzzle flashes. A second German drops, then a third, before they load their dead and wounded onto their shoulders and retreat down the hill.

A few days later the partisans hear that the Soviets are finally on the River Hron, then that they've taken Brusno. As Haim limps with

the lice-ridden fighters out of the forest and down into the valley, a heavy machine gun on his back, he falls under the weight and nearly breaks his knee. A comrade supports him for the rest of the descent. They find the town full of Red Army trucks and Russian troops. The fascists are gone. He has his first bath in 125 days.

IT'S THE END OF THE WAR, but the end is different than he imagined. The Soviets first march the partisans, their own allies, for days under guard in the Carpathians until they reach Poland. Many of the partisans are communists too, but the Soviets are paranoid, treating them like prisoners. It's so cold in the mountains that Haim's tears freeze on his eyelashes. At one mountain pass Haim comes across the body of a partisan he knows, a German anti-Nazi who'd fought in the communist ranks. The body is barefoot, and one of the Russian guards has the dead man's boots. "There is no such thing as a German communist," the guard explains.

The sorry contingent eventually trudges into the Polish town of Nowy Sącz, where the Soviets have commandeered a Franciscan monastery and set up a transit camp for liberated soldiers of the Western Allies. They quarter Haim with Albert, an American paratrooper who was captured on D-Day and somehow ended up in Soviet custody; a few Yugoslav fighters; and two RAF pilots, a Canadian and a Scot. The rags of his British uniform are thrown out, and he's issued the clean uniform of a Red Army soldier, with new underwear, boots, and a fur hat. A photograph survives of him in this outfit, lean but grinning.

While he waits for permission to move on, he tries to find the Jews of Nowy Sącz. There were eighteen thousand before the war. No one came to help them—no Allied commandos, no Jewish parachutists, no partisans, no one. No one bombed the rail lines or the camp at Belzec where they were gassed. The floors of their abandoned homes, he finds, were torn up after their departure by Polish peasants who'd been raised on legends of Jewish gold. He counts fifteen people still alive.

He's sent by train to the port of Odessa in Ukraine, where the Allies are processing returnees. He's given a toothbrush, cigarettes, soap, and a berth on a Dutch ship to liberated Naples. From there, he flies across the Mediterranean and finally lands back in Cairo.

It's been a year since he left. Tony Simonds is there to greet him. The reserved Englishman embraces him, Haim remembers, "with strange emotion, as if I'd come back from the land of the dead."

AT FIRST HE THINKS he'll see Haviva, along with Zvi and Rafi. He assumes he's the last to arrive of the four parachutists who shared rooms at the hotel in Banská Bystrica. When the camp was attacked, he thought they ran in a luckier direction and made it out before him. When he asks Simonds, the officer's response is vague.

At Shepheard's Hotel there's only one person waiting for him on the balcony—not a parachutist, but one of the senior Mossad men running the mission, Zvi Yehieli, who has come from Tel Aviv. The older man hugs the wraith who has risen from the grave.

Haim's wife and daughter are in good health. As for his three comrades, the Mossad man says—we'll talk about them later.

Haim asks if he's the last to return. No, the older man says. He's the first. The truth is that he's both the first and the last.

With some prodding, Haim begins to tell his story. He speaks for hours, into the next day, maybe the one after that, he isn't sure. He keeps telling the story after the war, then after the creation of the state of Israel three years later. When I speak to his two sons eighty years later, they remember their father sitting at his typewriter in the late 1960s, in one corner of their modest living room at the kibbutz, working on *Operation Amsterdam*. One of his sons, Rafi, is named for Rafi Reisz, who was imprisoned with Haviva and sent with her to the anti-tank ditch.

Haim doesn't think he's a hero and is embarrassed to be treated like one. He just doesn't want the details, or his friends, to be forgotten. He always saw the mission less as military than as instructive. It was an extension of his work in the Zionist youth movement, his son Rafi said, where you're taught to lead by example. And if the mission was a lesson for others, of course it must be written down.

Operation Amsterdam, which has served me so well in my excavation of this history, is out of print in Hebrew and was never translated into English, and beyond the small number of people who take an interest in the parachutists of 1944, the name of the author, Haim Hermesh, is unknown. He spent his life on the kibbutz doing whatever job was necessary, however menial, in the sublime style of the men and women who founded Israel. At Kibbutz Kfar Glikson there's a mural of him on the wall of a barn, but he's not armed or in uniform. He's in a sun hat, holding a giant zucchini. The scythe in the name he chose was always a simple farm tool. He lived to eighty-eight and died in 2007.

But in Cairo in April 1945, having made his unlikely escape, Haim is still young, his future uncertain, the last terrible year only beginning to cohere in his memory. He seems dazed and fragile. He jumped out of a plane in British uniform, surfaced in Soviet uniform, saw the destruction of the European world he came from, and will soon go home to a country that doesn't yet exist. The line between alive and dead is thin. He must be startled to be on one side and not the other, or even unsure which side he's really on.

The Mossad man debriefing him doesn't want to tell the truth about the others too quickly. But it can't be put off forever. Haviva is found in a British military cemetery in Prague as body No. 209, originally exhumed from a mass grave at Kremnička, Slovakia: "A woman of about 20-30 years old," according to the forensic report, "wearing a military shirt, trousers, a blue knitted sweater with a zipper, a water-resistant dark gray coat, yellow boots. Black hair." Cause of death: "The sign of a shot to the head." Her comrade Rafi is with her. The body of Zvi, her lover, is never found. Her beloved book, the one buried in the forest before the final battle, is exhumed by one of the survivors and returned to Haviva's kibbutz.

Haim is in Cairo on May 8, the sun roasting the roiling neighborhoods along the Nile. Suddenly civilians and soldiers flood the streets and a wave of noise crashes over the city. Going up a flight of stairs alone, he meets a jubilant mass of troops coming down. This war is over.

10

AFTERLIFE

When the parachutists' mission ends, Ada's mission begins. This is the girl Enzo met in school in Rome, with whom he left for the Land of Israel and built a new life at the kibbutz they founded together. Ada Sereni has spent the war at home with their three children.

Enzo is one of the millions of people missing in Europe in the spring of 1945. Many will never be found. Millions more are on the roads trying to get home, or to get as far from home as possible. The cover story is that Ada works for an organization dedicated to the welfare of Jewish soldiers in Italy. The real mission, which she's been given by her husband's comrades in the Mossad, is to run the clandestine ships bringing refugees to Palestine from Italian ports. But people's real missions are always complicated. She wants to find Enzo.

Ada's first stop is the headquarters of MI9 in Cairo. But the British know as little as anyone else, as is evident in a message from Billie Neville to her Mossad contacts around the same time. "I much regret that there is still no information on Dr. SERENI's location or his PW number," she writes. "From what I hear, ITALY seems to be in a chaotic state at the moment, with thousands of released PWs swarming toward the south; so I imagine it is enormously difficult to trace anyone just now."

The previous fall, Enzo was reported to be a prisoner of war, and several accounts placed him somewhere in the Russian occupation zone. There were also dubious flashes from places like Ferrara, where someone claimed to have spotted him at a prison camp. By the time British forces in northern Italy reached the camp in question, the prisoners had been evacuated and he was gone, if he'd been there at all.

Enzo's colleagues in Tel Aviv have been informed that he was seen alive after the jump, but was sent to the concentration camp at Dachau. They're not sure they should tell Ada. But they do, before she leaves, and one of the Mossad men writes to another, "There was no point in hiding anything from her."

Ada lands in Italy. Amid the masses of refugees and the ruined cities, she searches for prisoners newly released from the camps. First she hears that Enzo was seen at Mauthausen, in Austria. But soon she confirms that he was indeed sent to Dachau, next to Munich.

Her husband was at the camp, she discovers, by the fall of 1944. From the main facility he was transferred to a satellite camp at Mühldorf, where the Nazis had slave laborers building fortifications. Twenty days later he was returned to the main camp. She meets a former prisoner who claims to have seen Enzo at Dachau "in the special bloc for Englishmen, together with two British officers and a French captain, whose names I do not know."

AFTERLIFE

. . .

He's alive.

The telegram is in the files: "Enzo alive exhausted in hospital Russian zone Ada on way to him."

The message is from one of the Mossad men in Europe, relaying the news to Moshe Sharett, the future Israeli prime minister.

"Overwhelmed with joy Enzo's miraculous reemergence," responds Sharett, in the telegram's abbreviated wording. "Cable how was discovered all available details we all pray his recovery."

The news spreads in Palestine—a spark in the darkness of that year. The Jews are desperate for good news. Enzo's eldest daughter, Hagar, who is seventeen, has seen terrible photographs of people released from concentration camps, walking cadavers. She's happy her father is coming home but frightened to think what he looks like.

The chapters of Enzo's life at Dachau are recorded on a little card that I'm looking at right now.

When I reach the Dachau archive and speak to the patient researchers who work there, there's confusion at first about whether Enzo was in this camp at all. No one has heard of him. The problem is resolved when I think to check his alias, Capt. Shmuel Barda.

This name appears on an alphabetical list of prisoners who arrived on the same transport across the Alps from Italy. Among the *B*s I also find Bellotti and the priest Bonci, names familiar from the accounts both left of seeing Enzo. And here, the name printed neatly in a clerk's handwriting, is Barda—that is, Enzo himself.

In the nationality column he's listed as a solitary Englishman among Italians. He has given his hometown as Jerusalem—inaccurate, but maybe for him, in the national and religious sense, true. On his brown prisoner card I find that he told the SS his profession is "Prof. Philosophie." To the extent that it's possible to express one's humanity on an index card prepared by brutes who have stripped you, shaved you, and sprayed you with green disinfectant in a concrete hangar, Enzo succeeds.

According to the eyewitness Bellotti, Enzo was separated from the group after they arrived at Dachau, still in British uniform, then beaten by kapos on orders from the SS guards. He bore this with "great dignity" and kept up the spirits of his fellow prisoners in the weeks that followed, assuring them that the war was nearly over and that they would live.

I have never been to any of the Nazi camps, avoiding them deliberately. Victimhood is not my story, and I've always thought the Holocaust is a matter to be pondered by the people whose societies perpetrated it. As a result, I'm not expecting the evil of Dachau when I arrive. Evil rises from the ground, from the barracks, the crematorium, even from the bookshop at the entrance. It envelops everyone walking around with their smartphones, the groups of teenagers, the pair of solemn Australians who, on a backpacking trip through southern Germany, are visiting one of the must-see sites in their guidebook.

The little brown card chronicles the prisoner's transfer to the smaller camp at Mühldorf. From there, as a faint handwritten note informs me—or, rather, the archivist conversant in Nazi shorthand, who sits beside me and explains it—he's transferred back to the main camp on November 17, 1944. But he's not returned to the regular inmate population. Instead he's sent to a special facility for detention and interrogation known as the bunker. This low building still stands, and even after eighty years, even without the smells and sounds of prisoners and guards, it's a nightmare inside a nightmare. A dark corridor stretches past cell after cell beyond vision, the dominion of sadists—Johann Kick of the Gestapo, for example, who spent nine years plying his trade here, according to a label on the wall, before being executed by the Allies. Or the SS *Obersturmführer* Edgar Stiller, in charge of "special prisoners," sentenced to seven years for his crimes but released after only three.

Our special prisoner isn't here for long, just a day. Guards take him from the bunker across the camp to the low brick crematorium— I don't know in what condition. Prisoners were sometimes marched to the crematorium and hung from the rafters opposite the ovens as a matter of convenience. There's also a gas chamber in an adjoining room, but it doesn't seem to have been used. I don't know the details, just that on the left side of the neat little card documenting the final chapters of Enzo—someone who dreamed of capturing the spirit of his time in a great and sweeping novel—a black Germanic cross is visible next to a date.

After months of sleuthing, Ada is grasping the incredible news of Enzo's survival when she finds this same card. Someone explains to her what the cross means, just as it is explained to me. Her final telegram on this matter is sent from Milan.

"Happy news completely false. Enzo was killed in Dachau on 18 November."

OUT OF THE SKY

. . .

When she sends this telegram in October 1945, Enzo has been dead for almost a year. He died eleven days after Hannah and two days before Haviva.

Two months pass.

It's nighttime on Christmas Eve 1945, off the coast of western Galilee. The crew of a battered freighter acquired by the Mossad in Genoa slip her through the screen of British destroyers and approach the beach with 252 refugees on board. The British troops who should be on patrol are probably drunk in their quarters. The only people on the beach are Jewish underground fighters waiting in the dark. When I meet one of them years later, in his nineties, he describes this as a "night of terrors."

The freighter runs aground. The fighters are struggling out into the choppy sea to bring the refugees ashore, in rowboats and on their backs, when the ship takes on water and begins to capsize. Two women who survived the war in Europe and nearly reached the promised land are drowned within sight of the shore. The rest arrive shivering on the sand. The Hebrew poet Nathan Alterman publishes a poem in the newspaper mocking the British in verse, declaring this to be a naval triumph on par with Trafalgar. The ship is the *Hannah Senesh*.

She went a young woman, a promising poet, and came back a capsized freighter—is there comfort in this? For the damaged people on board, and for their thousands of Israeli children and grandchildren, I think the answer is yes. They are borne to their new lives by Hannah Senesh, that is, by people who believe in shared fate, who respond to disaster not with evasion or paralysis but with dramatic action. Soon another 343 refugees make it to the coast aboard the *Haviva Reick*.

It's Ada who is sending the ships from Italy. Ada the Mossad operator, whose talents for persuasion and subterfuge are noted by officials and clerks around the liberated ports—not the private Ada, a widow who grieves for her husband and pines for her children. It's this second Ada who writes to the children from Milan a week after the *Hannah Senesh* reaches Palestine, on the last day of 1945.

Their father Enzo, she writes, "on whom I leaned for 25 years," is gone. The three of them are growing up and will soon leave home. "A 40-year-old woman is progressing toward the end and can't waste years. She must change her life. And I know I must change my life."

She's explaining to the children, or maybe to herself, why she left them to save strangers, to bring people she has never met to a place where they can be home. Is she escaping the personal into the national or the mythic? Decades later, one of Enzo's grandsons, a historian, will ask his mother about his grandfather the hero, whom he never met. He seems to have caught her at an unguarded moment. What her father did, she says, was selfish.

I don't know what Ada thinks in 1945, only what she writes. "I don't want to become an angry, bitter woman who burdens her children and everyone around her. This is my last chance to do it. Afterward it will be too late."

These sentiments aren't detectable in the memoir she publishes later about her exploits in Italy. Her book tells a national story in which Jews are people of action, not victims, and she is the protagonist, not a woman afflicted by sorrow. Maybe she falls in love with her Mossad partner in Italy, as some of their colleagues always believe, and which would be human, or maybe she doesn't. She'll never say, and it's not important. Grief and love are private matters. "These thoughts about my innermost self," she writes home in her letter, "the great effort I'm making to find a fulcrum for my life instead of the one I lost—this I'm writing to you, children, and to no one else."

Nine days later, at the Italian port of Vado Ligure, 908 refugees set sail for the homeland aboard the freighter *Enzo Sereni*.

I GO TO MOUNT HERZL in Jerusalem, the national military cemetery, forty-five minutes from my street by bus and tram. I feel that there must be another portal into this story, some essence I've missed. Maybe it's here.

The cemetery is always growing. As I work on this book, hundreds of new graves are added to the thousands already there among stone paths and cypresses, including several that belong to people I knew, who were alive when I began my research. If you visit now, you'll see young people visiting the graves of friends killed in the most recent war, and parents at the graves of children, the uniform military headstones adorned with photographs, flags, and flowers—the more death there is in the cemetery, the more life is drawn to the cemetery. In one of the oldest sections there's a special plot for the parachutists.

AFTERLIFE

Hannah is here, and has been since 1950, with the arrival of another ship from Europe. This one belongs to the new Israeli Navy, which is just two years old, like the state. A crowd gathers at the Haifa docks to watch a casket descend the gangway, and then an army truck sets out across the country, down streets lined with citizens. It's the most elaborate state funeral yet held here, bar one—that of Theodor Herzl, the journalist and playwright who wrote *The Jewish State* and convened the first Zionist Congress. His remains were brought a year earlier and reinterred on this same hill in Jerusalem, which is named for him. The two writers from Budapest, born on either side of the Danube, are now divided by a few steps in this city where neither of them lived. As their lives played out from beginning to end, between their city and mine, both of them dreamed of writing the great play or novel but never did. Instead, they enacted their dramas in the world.

Outside the small museum named for Hannah at her kibbutz is a sculpture commissioned in her memory by the Zionist movement after her execution. It was originally placed at the Rákoskeresztúr Cemetery in Budapest, where she was first buried before being brought to Israel. The sculpture followed her here much later. The artist depicts a figure that isn't Hannah, or any recognizable person, but a generic and faceless woman, only the back of her head visible as she steps into the stone out of which she is carved. It's the beginning of Hannah's transformation from a young person of flesh and blood into a symbol that is larger than life and shorn of life. Now she belongs to Zionism.

Some parts of her diary, where she seems despondent or disillusioned, are smoothed over before publication, like her declaration of hatred for menial labor, for example, which is honest but ideologically deficient. "I know that I won't be a simple worker. I can't be and don't want to be," becomes merely, "I think I won't be a simple worker." The new state needs her to be the perfect Hebrew fighter, a tireless worker of indomitable grin and twinkling eyes, author of the immortal anthem "Eli Eli." She's a hero in an age when the response to heroes is to aspire to their example, not to suspect their motives or suppress discomfort at our own inadequacy by tearing them down to our size. The hero Hannah Senesh is not an immigrant vulnerable to longing and regret, but a pure daughter of Israel. Her mother is the nation.

Actually, when the sculpture is unveiled at the cemetery in Budapest at the war's end, her real mother is standing there, having escaped a death march and hidden for months in a monastery. When Katherine returns to the family home, she finds it looted and ruined. Like her daughter's body, she won't be in Europe much longer, and will soon be leaving for Israel to join her son, Gyuri, who now goes by the Hebrew name Giora. In the 1958 play *Hannah Senesh*, performed by Israel's national theater, the martyr asks her mother if she made the right choice. "Of course, Aniko, of course!" answers Katherine. "Could you have done otherwise?" But her real mother never said any such thing.

Next to Hannah in the Israeli military cemetery is Haviva. You could be excused for thinking they're together again, but the two heroines of the mission seem never to have met when they were alive. By the time Haviva began training, Hannah had already jumped.

Haviva too was retrieved from her European grave and buried here, though with less fanfare. She was perhaps the most effective of all the parachutists, in practical terms—but practical terms were not the important ones. Hannah's writing and story were better, or at least more useful to the storytellers, and she was free of the personal complications of her older comrade.

The name Enzo Sereni appears on another marker a few paces away, but the grave is empty. The remains of the Italian are presumably under the pretty garden planted atop the ash heap at the Dachau crematorium, mixed with the remains of twenty-five thousand other people.

THE CEMETERY PLOT would be more complete with a mention of Egon Roth. Maybe there could be a plaque with words from his oration at the Národný Dom hotel in the mission's final days:

> You brag about how you stand tall, as if you came here as representatives of some master race from the land of Israel. You must know: We're not ashamed to hide and grovel, escape and sneak across borders in order to save one more Jew from this giant tomb. For years we've been grateful for every day that passes, and have been planning tricks to move each of us one step closer to the Land of Israel, and suddenly a few "heroes" get up, get on a plane, and jump into the open grave.

I don't mean this to be the final verdict, just one commentary, words that make room for the uncertainty surrounding the operation and human fate in general. Egon is worth remembering, even if he wasn't a parachutist. He was killed at the camp in the forest a few weeks later. No one knows where he's buried, or if he was buried at all.

The official grave site of the parachutists in Jerusalem is too neat and too static to contain this story, and a cemetery too final a setting for these characters. Their plot has been ordered too obviously in service of a national saga, the graves arranged in the shape of a *V*, maybe for victory. Or it might be a formation of migrating birds, which does feel right.

NOT FAR FROM THE CEMETERY is an ordinary spot in this city, a sidewalk where a flight of outdoor steps meets a residential street. I spend some time loitering. The steps are a pedestrian path named for Hannah, and the street is named for Enzo.

An elderly woman passes with a dog. A young woman with a double stroller, two kids hypnotized by little screens, stray cats. I think about Hannah and Enzo waiting in Bari for her infiltration flight, arguing about the existence of God.

I've lived most of my life in this country, where the language of the Bible is the language of electricity bills and pop music, where Jews aren't forced into questions of identity or warped by the fantasies of their neighbors, where children grow up thinking Christianity is an obscure minority religion. My kids were born here and think all of it is unremarkable, that things have always been this way.

The people whose names appear on the street signs dreamed of this state and helped will it into being. But they never got to live here. They were never issued a parking ticket in Hebrew, or barbecued in a crowded park on Independence Day. I've met Enzo's granddaughter, but he never did. This doesn't seem fair. I ride my bike across town a few times to the intersection of Enzo and Hannah, hoping for something evocative to happen. But it's just a quiet street, and nothing ever does.

FOR A WHILE I become convinced that the secret spirit of this story may lie in a single overlooked sentence in one of the books on my shelf.

The revelation appears at the very end of the authorized collection of Hannah's writing, *Diaries, Poems, Testimonies*, where it's presented without source or explanation. Deep in the forests of northern Yugoslavia, in modern-day Croatia, a box was buried containing Hannah's possessions from the final months of her life— and possibly writing that no one has ever seen. There's no mention of who buried this box. The author, an Israeli historian who was among the first editors to compile Hannah's writing, informs us only that it has never been found. I want to ask him if he knows more, but he died in 1961.

This tantalizing lead initiates a burst of internet research in which I watch a video titled "Metal Detecting in Croatia" and find that the necessary gear is available for purchase at Gorazd Orozim S.P. in the town of Prebold. But is Hannah's box even made of metal? If it exists, which seems unlikely?

This box can only remain an enigma, like Hemingway's missing novel of the First World War, the one his wife misplaced on a train from Paris. Of this manuscript the author once said he wished there were surgery that could erase his memory of what had been lost.

OUT OF THE SKY

. . .

THE VISTA EXPANDS and the inland sea shrinks as the airplane strains up to nine thousand feet. Wind roars past the open door. There's a sharp smell of fuel. Over the engine's whine a voice shouts—ready.

The heart of the story might lie in the space between an airplane and the ground. Or maybe in the mad act of entrusting one's life to fabric and rope. A friend, a former paratrooper, said it's wrong to write a book about parachutists without jumping. These considerations made sense this morning in the car from Jerusalem to the closest parachute school I found online, a two-hour drive through the Judean desert. But the reasons evaporate now as the little white plane pitches, as the instructor clamps onto the back of my harness and I sit with my feet out the door.

The sandwich and cocoa from the airfield at Bari in 1944 somehow stir in my own stomach, though I've been mindful of Haim's example and have eaten little. Below there's no great European forest. Instead, it's the expanse of barren mountains in Israel and the Hashemite Kingdom of Jordan, a valley running between them directly below the plane. In the valley is the Dead Sea, split into channels and pools that are deep blue in the middle and shimmering turquoise around the edge—but for a few seconds I see nothing because I'm falling and my eyes are screwed shut.

When the parachute opens, I find myself floating gently between two archetypes.

Far below and to the right, standing out from the cliffs that line the western shore of the sea, is the flat top of Masada. The ruins of King Herod's palace on the hilltop are easily visible from this altitude, even after two millennia. So are the remains of the square camps built by Roman troops who besieged the Jewish rebels in the palace during the revolt of 70 CE. When the legionnaires moved up the siege tower to breach the walls, the Jews famously drew lots and killed one another, the last man killing himself, choosing death over slavery. This is the myth of Masada, one celebrated in Israel's early years before people grew out of it. I've never cared for the legend myself. The men, women, and children on the hill left us no poems or prayers, none of their own words at all, and the only account comes from a Jewish turncoat writing history for the Romans. There's no human face to this story, and nothing comes of their act. Everyone dies, and the empire wins. The suicide is sterile.

On the opposite side of the valley below my feet is a second line of hills. Among them is Nebo—one of the most famous mountains in literature, even if I don't know exactly which one it is and doubt anyone does. The epic recorded in the Five Books of Moses, the Torah, begins with the creation of the world and ends on Mount Nebo.

Moses is a Hebrew boy raised as a prince in the royal court of Egypt while his people are enslaved and slaughtered by their overlords, their infant sons drowned in the Nile. They've been slaves for four hundred years. He can close his eyes and continue his life in the palace, but instead he kills an Egyptian overseer and escapes to the desert. He's safe. But then God speaks to him from a burning bush, telling him to go back. Moses doesn't have an army, in fact he's alone, but he goes. He must somehow bring the Israelites out of slavery to their home, to a place that neither he nor they have ever seen. For forty years he leads them through the wilderness before finally reaching this very ridge, the border of Canaan. He won't be going farther.

The story ends on Mount Nebo, where he stands by himself and looks over the promised land—"from Gilead to Dan, all of Naftali, the land of Efraim and Manasseh, the entire land of Judah until the western sea, the south, the plain of the valley of Jericho, city of palm trees, until Tzo'ar." It's a beautiful place, the same one I see from up here in the sky. In the biblical scene the mountain is like a stage. A single figure stands with his back to the audience, the lights about to dim. The final words of the Torah remind us that this character not only achieved great deeds but did so "in the eyes of all of Israel"—that this was power not exercised through unseen influence or enacted by decree, but performed. He showed the people who he was and who they could be, and showed them where to go.

The strange and lingering power of the parachutists lies not in any military victory, but in the older stories pulsing beneath the surface of theirs. The hero escapes danger but returns. She's given new words and actions. She'll be remembered. She stands on the mountain and is allowed a glimpse of what happens next. But she won't cross. Her part is over.

NOTES ON SOURCES

Among the many sources that made this book possible, I'd like to acknowledge five published works that were indispensable.

The first is Haim Hermesh's memoir, *Mivtza Amsterdam* (Operation Amsterdam), from 1971, now out of print. Although the book exists only in Hebrew, for the ease of the reader in English I've translated the title throughout, as I've done with other recurring titles of Hebrew books. It would have been impossible to bring the mission to life without the writing of this sensitive survivor. The second work is *The Emissary: A Life of Enzo Sereni* by Ruth Bondy, first published in Hebrew in 1973 and released in English translation in 1977. The third is *Haviva Reick: A Kibbutz Pioneer's Mission and Fall Behind Nazi Lines* by Tehila Ofer and Zeev Ofer, published in Hebrew in 2004 and in English in 2014. The fourth book is the memoir by parachutist Joel Palgi, *Ruakh Gedola Ba'a* (A Great Wind Cometh). First published in Hebrew in 1946, the title is drawn from the Book of Job. The English edition from 2003, translated by the author's widow, Phyllis Palgi, is titled *Into the Inferno: The Memoir of a Jewish Paratrooper Behind Nazi Lines*. And finally, the standard collection of writing by, and testimonies about, Hannah, first published after WWII and still in print after fifteen Hebrew editions: *Hannah Szenes: Yomanim Shirim Eduyot* (Hannah Szenes: Diaries, Poems, Testimonies). A condensed English version, published in 1971, is titled *Hannah Senesh: Her Life and*

NOTES ON SOURCES

Diary. In the source notes I refer to the book simply as *Diaries*. For clarity and the ease of the reader, I've chosen to render Hannah's family name, Szenes, as "Senesh," the phonetic spelling that became the most common version of the name in English, even in cases when the Hungarian spelling appears in the original source.

With few exceptions, I've used the Hebrew originals of the above works, and the translations that appear here are mine. Hannah's diary entries from before 1940, written in Hungarian, were translated for me by Agnes Kende from Hannah's original handwritten journals, which have been scanned and made available online by Israel's National Library in Jerusalem. The excerpts from Hannah's writing appear courtesy of the Szenes Family Archive, with thanks to Ori and Mirit Eisen, the National Library of Israel collections. I'm grateful to the library for making this important material accessible to the public and for permission to quote from the diaries, and to Dr. Hezi Amiur for his help in navigating the collection.

I'd also like to acknowledge an MA thesis by Rakefet Dayan: "Between Hannah and St. Joan: Hannah Szenes in image and reality" (Haifa University, 2007). Dayan's Hebrew thesis, one of the most valuable sources I encountered on the subject of Hannah and her mythic afterlife, has unfortunately never been published.

1. THE SCYTHE

The description of Haim's jump, and the personal account as seen through Haim's eyes in the following pages, is drawn from his Hebrew memoir *Mivtza Amsterdam* (Operation Amsterdam). Additional information is from an early essay by Haim written immediately after the war, "A Camp of Jewish Fighters," in *Magen Baseter* (Secret Defender), an important collection of first-person accounts documenting Zionist underground activities in WWII (1948, edited by Zerubabel Gilad). Further details of Haim's mission are from documents in the Hagana Historical Archives, Eliyahu

NOTES ON SOURCES

Golomb House, Tel Aviv. I'm grateful to archive staffers Orly Levy and Shimri Salomon for their patient assistance. Details from modern Bari, Italy, are from a visit in the spring of 2024.

The theory about the *"weedy looking, delicate, shy type of people"* is drawn from the unpublished memoir by Tony Simonds (Lt. Col. Anthony Simonds OBE), *Pieces of War*. The manuscript, completed in 1979, is now held by the Imperial War Museum, London. I'm grateful to the IWM staff for their assistance.

the first shots the British fired in anger in World War II, on September 2, 1939: Bernard Wasserstein, *Britain and the Jews of Europe, 1939–1945* (Oxford University Press, 1988).

worm-eaten and useless: This incident is described in *Mivtza Amsterdam*.

"They're as dangerous as the Nazis.": The comment, from parachutist Aryeh Fichman, is recorded by Haim in *Mivtza Amsterdam*.

"were not around long enough to leave a record of their existence and they vanished without a trace": Eric Morris in *Guerrillas in Uniform*, cited in Judith Tydor Baumel-Schwartz, *Perfect Heroes: The World War II Parachutists and the Making of Israeli Collective Memory* (University of Wisconsin Press, 2010).

Major McAdam, the Frenchman with a false Scottish name, is mentioned in *Mivtza Amsterdam* and also in the unpublished memoir by Simonds, who describes his defection from Vichy forces on the Lebanon-Palestine border and recalls him as a "French Maquis from Martinique." According to Simonds, "We never knew his real name."

The partisans' truck that ran on logs is mentioned (and appears in a photograph) in the Hebrew volume *Tzankhanei Ha-tikva* (Parachutists of Hope), published in 1995, edited by Gershon Rivlin, Rehavam Amir, and Shmuel Stempler.

NOTES ON SOURCES

The clandestine meeting in Tel Aviv is recounted in Tuvia Friling, *Arrows in The Dark: David Ben-Gurion, the Yishuv Leadership, and Rescue Attempts During the Holocaust* (University of Wisconsin Press, 2005, Hebrew original published 1998), the definitive account of the Zionist movement's attempts to save Jews and combat Nazi Germany in WWII. An account of the scene appears in *Mivtza Amsterdam*.

The conflicting reports about Hannah's whereabouts in June, July, and August 1944 can be found in the mission files at the Hagana Historical Archives. The report that Hannah had boarded the train was delivered to her comrade Reuven Dafni by a partisan named Maté shortly after the partisan escorted her to the border. Different reports in the archive mistakenly place Hannah in Budapest, at large and operational, on June 20, July 15, July 19, and July 28.

"the young British officer smart in her army uniform": From Reuven Dafni's Hebrew essay "The Last Border," which first appeared in 1948 in *Magen Baseter* (Secret Defender), and a version of which appears in the Hannah Senesh anthology *Diaries*. I've relied on the latter version.

The letter from the Canadian major William Jones, with his description of Hannah, is in the Hagana Historical Archives, dated November 2, 1944.

2. HANNAH

"Agrees to any job.": From Hannah's agent file in the Hagana Historical Archives, entry dated November 14, 1943.

This description of Enzo is drawn mainly from Ruth Bondy's *The Emissary*. Though written in the hagiographic period of Israeli history and with admiration for the subject, Bondy's book doesn't ignore Enzo's flaws. The reference to his drinking, for example, while posted as an envoy to the persecuted Jews of Iraq: "In his requests for liquor he stressed that he needed it for various social activities on behalf of the movement, but it was evident that he needed it also for himself."

NOTES ON SOURCES

There was an episode in the late 1930s in which he became infatuated with a seventeen-year-old named Lonnie, whom he met in Königsberg, Germany. He confessed his love to no effect, according to Bondy, "and he was brokenhearted."

"The dangers of the mission are clear to you": Hermesh, *Mivtza Amsterdam*.

"The day after tomorrow I'm starting something new": Hannah's letter to her brother, Gyuri (Giora), December 25, 1943, in *Diaries*.

"I'm glad I've grown lately": Hannah's diary, October 7, 1934, translated from the handwritten original in Hungarian by Agnes Kende (along with the rest of the Hungarian entries from before 1939, when Hannah's writing moves mostly to Hebrew). In some places the published diaries in both English and Hebrew diverge significantly from Hannah's original text. The diaries, with the rest of Hannah's papers and photographs, are kept at Israel's National Library in Jerusalem.

"We got our class reunion rings today.": Hannah's diary, National Library, April 27, 1935.

"I wrote only two poems all summer": Hannah's diary, National Library, August 29, 1935.

"Tuesday, the 22nd, was the premiere of a film": Hannah's diary, National Library, October 25, 1935.

"I wrote the play and directed it": Hannah's diary, National Library, April 19, 1936.

"Just to note that Gyuri": Hannah's diary, National Library, May 9, 1936.

"My desire, still and always, is to be a writer": Hannah's diary, National Library, August 3, 1936.

"At first the beach seemed terribly tiny": Hannah's diary, National Library, July 19, 1937.

"The play, Sweet Home, *was quite weak"*: Hannah's diary, National Library, January 1, 1938.

"The events have caused indescribable tumult for us as well.": Hannah's diary, National Library, March 13, 1938.

NOTES ON SOURCES

In a train compartment the following month: Hannah's diary, National Library, April 24, 1938.

"I've become a Zionist.": Hannah's diary, National Library, October 27, 1938.

Hannah's description of the horticulture class at Nahalal is from her diary, April 10, 1940. Her vow not to be a simple worker is quoted in Rakefet Dayan, "Between Hannah and St. Joan: Hannah Szenes in image and reality" (Master's thesis, Haifa University, 2007).

"Nothing I do makes any sense": *Diaries*, April 12, 1941.

Joel Palgi's description of meeting Hannah in Tel Aviv is from his 1946 memoir, *Ruakh Gedola Ba'a* (A Great Wind Cometh).

"After taking the elevator up": Hannah's diary, National Library, June 21, 1937.

records seeing a performance of Rigoletto: This is Haviva, who saw the opera with Zvi Ben-Yaakov in the late summer or early fall of 1944. They also saw *The Barber of Seville*. From the biography *Haviva Reick* by Tehila Ofer and Zeev Ofer.

"The marvelous daughter of a nobleman!": This exchange appears in Palgi's *Ruakh Gedola Ba'a* (A Great Wind Cometh).

"Greetings to you Sereni!": This letter from Hannah to Enzo is in the Hagana Historical Archives, dated December 15, 1943.

"During the quest": The book by the two American psychologists is George R. Goethals and Scott T. Allison, *The Romance of Heroism and Heroic Leadership* (Emerald Publishing Limited, 2019).

"Opposing him with clear, penetrating logic was 22-year-old Hannah": From Dafni's essay "The Last Border," in *Diaries*.

"Her face glowed and she radiated cheer": Dafni, "The Last Border," *Diaries*.

"our Joan of Arc": From the documentary film *Blessed Is the Match*, written by Sophie Sartain and Roberta Grossman, directed by Roberta Grossman, 2008.

NOTES ON SOURCES

"Remember, only he who wants to die dies!": Dafni, "The Last Border," Diaries.

"Let it open above me, let it open!": *Shiro shel Tzankhan* (Paratrooper's Song) by Yoram Taharlev, 1969.

"that beautiful land of mountains and forests": Dafni, "The Last Border," Diaries.

"A few interesting and beautiful things have happened to me, but I must wait before I can tell you.": Hannah's letter from Yugoslavia to her brother Gyuri, dated May 10, 1944, in the Hagana Historical Archives.

The book by the Hungarian leader, with the scene from the Austrian castle in March 1944, is *Memoirs*, by Admiral Nicholas Horthy, Regent of Hungary, published in London in 1956. The precise number of Hungarian Jews deported to the death camps, according to the Reich plenipotentiary in Hungary, Edmund Veesenmayer, was 437,402 between May 14 and July 9, 1944. See, for example, Eleonore Lappin, "The Death Marches of Hungarian Jews Through Austria in the Spring of 1945," *Yad Vashem Studies* 28 (2000): 203–42, www.yadvashem.org/articles/academic/the-death-marches-of-hungarian-jews-through-austria.html.

"regarding the internal structure of our units": The intercepted note from Commissar Ivan H. Šibl can be found, in Hebrew translation, in the Hagana Historical Archives.

"The meeting is next to the Catholic church in M.S. at precisely 12:00 and 17:00 as the bell tolls.": Hagana Historical Archives, May 29, 1944.

"taking a special interest in Hannah Senesh.": March 26, 1944, in the Hagana Historical Archives. His full name is given as Michael Boroz.

3. BUDAPEST

"Often I think this city is like a cheap hotel in a back alley": This quote from Gyula Krúdy, describing Budapest around the time of WWI, is from

NOTES ON SOURCES

Victor Sebestyen, *Budapest: Portrait of a City Between East and West* (Pantheon Books, 2022).

"Shot through the nape.": The translation of this quote from Radnóty's last poem is from Sebestyen's *Budapest*.

The notebook with Hannah's reading list is kept at the National Library in Jerusalem.

"Her eyes no longer shone.": From Joel Palgi's essay "How She Fell," *Diaries*.

"unusual girl": Dafni, "The Last Border," *Diaries*.

The typed testimony from Jacques Antoine Tissandier, code name Ivan, is in the Hagana Historical Archives.

"The Drava flows between hills that rise high": Hannah's diary, National Library, June 18, 1937.

Mala Subotica: The town's name, and the details of the currency Hannah carried, is from testimony from Dafni dated June 26, 1945, in the Hagana Historical Archives. The episode involving the partisan guide who brought the last written message from Hannah is mentioned in the same report. The text of the note is in the Hagana Historical Archives, along with other documents from an investigation conducted by Hagana officials in June 1945, a year after Hannah's disappearance on the border.

The note from Hannah passed on by the partisan, dated June 9, 1944, is in the Hagana Historical Archives.

4. HEADQUARTERS

"Dressed like a pirate, looked like a pirate, and in another age would have been a pirate" and other quotes from Simonds's unpublished *Pieces of War*, from the typewritten manuscript kept at the Imperial War Museum. For additional information on the remarkable Simonds, I'm grateful to Raymond Simonds, keeper of the Simonds family website (www.simondsfamily.me.uk), and to Simonds's daughter, Rosey Woollcombe..

NOTES ON SOURCES

The quotes from British officials regarding the recruitment of Jews are from Wasserstein's *Britain and the Jews of Europe*.

"swarming with diplomats, spies, refugees, and intelligence merchants": Barry Rubin, *Istanbul Intrigues: A True-Life Casablanca* (McGraw-Hill Publishing Company, 1989). Rubin's book is also the source for the details here about the Dogwood affair as it relates to the OSS office in Istanbul.

The connection between Dogwood and the Zionist office in Istanbul was unraveled by Tuvia Friling and published in his book *Arrows in the Dark*. I interviewed Friling at his home in southern Israel in February 2024.

She's to say "Merhavia," the name of a kibbutz: Hagana Historical Archives, August 22, 1944.

5. ENZO

A version of this chapter's opening, about Holocaust literature, appeared in an article I wrote for *The Free Press* ("We Misunderstood the Nazis," July 10, 2024).

"Enzo was indeed one of the most dramatic figures in our movement": This quote from Moshe Sharett is from his introduction to *Ha-Aviv Ha-Kadosh* (The Sacred Spring), a collection of Enzo's writings published in Hebrew (Am Oved, 1969).

The exchange between Enzo and Joel about writing a book appears in Joel's 1946 memoir.

"Since then no Jew openly appears on the streets": Bondy, *The Emissary*.

only fifteen live to see the end of the war, one of them Settimia Spizzichino: John Cornwell, *Hitler's Pope: The Secret History of Pius XII* (Viking Penguin, 1999).

Enzo chooses his own drop zone from a tourist map, where he spots a place called Campo di Hanibale: Bondy, *The Emissary*.

NOTES ON SOURCES

The name of Enzo's companion, Rosselli Lorenzo del Turco, is from *The Emissary*. A report from del Turco himself can be found in the Hagana Historical Archives, without his name, dated October 18, 1944, communicated to the Hagana by Wing Cmdr. Dennis of MI9.

Enzo's renunciation of pacifism while traveling through Sinai is described in *The Emissary*. This happened immediately after he signed up for the British war effort in 1940, as he was brought to Cairo to begin his service.

"the call for such sacrifices is always a deception": Bondy, *The Emissary*.

"a revolution of the soul": This quote from Yaakov Zur, writing in 1974, can be found in the files related to the parachutists' mission in the Central Zionist Archives in Jerusalem. It's also Zur who suggested that a better title for his friend's biography would be *The Apostle*.

"You must preach the Gospel at all times, and when necessary use words": This quote from St. Francis appears in Richard Rohr, *Eager to Love: The Alternative Way of Francis of Assisi* (Franciscan Media, 2014).

"If something has happened to require my return, write what it is.": Dated April 4, 1944, in the Central Zionist Archives. Moshe Sharett also wrote, on March 23, 1944, urging him not to jump.

"There was no replacement for Enzo.": David Ben-Gurion, quoted in *The Emissary*.

"I'm going in the hope that I'll make some small contribution": This letter appears in *Arrows in the Dark*, Hebrew edition, translation mine.

"And if not": This letter appears in *Tzankhanei Ha-tikva* (Parachutists of Hope).

In 1942, for example, while engaged in underground Zionist work in Iraq: Bondy, *The Emissary*.

The description of del Turco's escape is from his testimony communicated to the Hagana men by Wing Cmdr. Dennis of MI9 on October 18, 1944. In the Hagana Historical Archives.

NOTES ON SOURCES

The professor who sees Enzo in prison in Verona is Giovanni Dean. From *The Emissary*.

"*I want to get to know this century of ours inside and out.*": Etty Hillesum, *An Interrupted Life and Letters from Westerbork* (Picador, 1996).

"*The worst survived, that is, the fittest*": Primo Levi, *The Drowned and the Saved* (Simon & Schuster, 1988).

A testimony from Bellotti can be found in an Italian document at the Dachau archive, titled: "A testimony given by Ermanno Bellotti to Giovanni Melodia about Dr. Enzo Sereni (aka Capt. Samuel Barda), Milan, June 7, 1961," translated for me by Rocco Blume. Bellotti mentions Don Mauro Bonci, a priest from Desio, near Milan, as one of the prisoners with them on the shipment from Bolzano. The priest's testimony about Enzo's mood and his biblical knowledge is cited in *The Emissary*.

"*We passed the Brenner at midday of the second day and everyone stood up*": Primo Levi, *Survival in Auschwitz* (The Orion Press, 1959), published in the original Italian in 1947.

Details of my train ride over the Alps, and of the Dachau camp in Germany, are from a research trip in April 2024.

The story told by the inmate David Pur, from Kibbutz Netzer Sereni, is from a short testimony included in *Tzankhanei Ha-tikva* (Parachutists of Hope).

6. HAVIVA

The Kibbutz Maanit archive is run by the dedicated Rina Bareket, who assisted me in July 2024.

Ha-haverot Ba-kibbutz (Members of the Kibbutz) was published in 1943, edited by M. Poznanski and M. Schori. There is no English translation.

"*The fields of Beit She'an are grooved with many paths.*": This essay in the collection, whose author is named only as Yonina, is dated 1937.

NOTES ON SOURCES

Haviva's agent card is in the Hagana Historical Archives.

Lawson's assessment of Haviva is in the Hagana Historical Archives, dated March 19, 1944.

"I'm writing you these lines from a very beautiful place": Letter from Haviva, April 29, 1944, in the Maanit archive.

She notes the deafening noise of the streets: Letter from Haviva, May 5, 1944, Maanit archive.

Details of Haviva's relationships can be found in the biography *Haviva Reick* and are referenced in her letters in the Maanit archive. Her meeting in Cairo with the capitalist Arison is described in a letter from April 26, 1944.

"Everyone here did what they had to": This is archivist Rina Bareket.

"We're people with weaknesses": Letter from Haviva, May 16, 1944, Maanit archive.

"We're getting old, my girl": Letter from Haviva, June 22, 1944, Maanit archive.

"My work requires optimism, great strength, and good nerves.": Letter from Haviva, June 22, 1944, Maanit archive.

"In normal conditions, I know I wouldn't find this much patience for another person.": Letter from Haviva, August 6, 1944, Maanit archive.

"You may wonder why I'm writing to you unexpectedly": Ofer and Ofer, *Haviva Reick*.

The scene involving Michal, the pregnant wife of Zvi Ben-Yaakov, appears in *Haviva Reick*, and Haim describes it in *Mivtza Amsterdam*.

"We must parachute into Europe": Ofer and Ofer, *Haviva Reick*.

"We have been transferred to General Government, formerly Poland.": Postcard dated August 4, 1942, from *Haviva Reick*.

The report on the destruction of Slovak Jewry is in the Hagana Historical Archives, dated July 11, 1944.

NOTES ON SOURCES

"millions of Jews have been murdered and killed with asphyxiating gas": The panicked letter from two Zionist officials in Bratislava, Slovakia, dated April 12, 1944, is in the Hagana Historical Archives.

The files reveal other plans to be executed if feasible: Hagana document dated August 9, 1944, in the Hagana Historical Archives.

"We checked the situation here": Hagana communication dated August 30, 1944, in the Hagana Historical Archives.

"Her world seemed to have collapsed": Hermesh, *Mivtza Amsterdam*.

"Haviva, understand, there's no point in endangering a girl in this way": Hagana communication dated August 30, 1944, in the Hagana Historical Archives.

"efforts must be made to find a way for Haviva": Hagana communication dated August 14, 1944, in the Hagana Historical Archives.

"There's no rule that says not to use women in combat operations": Letter attributed to Alfai, dated August 16, 1944, in the Hagana Historical Archives.

"Has Karl arrived?": Hermesh, *Mivtza Amsterdam*.

The presence of reporter Joseph Morton on the same airplane as Haviva is noted in a report in the Hagana Historical Archives from August 1, 1945. Included in the file is an AP clipping: "Morton had accompanied a mission of Americans and British which flew into Slovakia in October to help bring out American airmen stranded there. The entire group was shot and their bodies cremated."

I visited the Tri Duby airfield and the town of Banská Bystrica with tour guide and historian Moshe Harmatz in August 2024.

"The huge black mass of the plane passed over my head": This quote, and details of Haim's jump into Slovakia, are from *Mivtza Amsterdam* and from Haim's early essay in *Magen Baseter* (Secret Defender). The date and unplanned altitude of the jump (2,000 meters) are given in a letter from the four parachutists in Banská Bystrica to commanders, dated September 26, 1944, in the Hagana Historical Archives.

NOTES ON SOURCES

his transformation into a Soviet "collaborator": From the same letter from the agents in Banská Bystrica, September 26, 1944, in the Hagana Historical Archives.

"I saw in assimilation a chance for the disappearance of anti-Semitism.": Juraj Špitzer, *I Did Not Want to Be a Jew*, edited by Thomas Gral (Dorrance Publishing Company, 1997), published in the original Slovak in 1994. Gral first met Špitzer in the Nováky concentration camp in 1943, before Gral was deported to Auschwitz; they met again fifty-two years later, as old men, to work on the translation.

"A-Force Amsterdam turned up.": Ofer and Ofer, *Haviva Reick*.

"By the time we found her": Letter from the parachutists to headquarters, September 26, 1944, in the Hagana Historical Archives.

The testimony from Dr. Tibor Tyroler is in the Hagana Historical Archives. The precise date is unclear, but it was apparently written after the end of the war in 1945.

"My situation is obviously quite critical": Letter from Haviva in Banská Bystrica to Hagana commanders, September 29, 1944, in the Hagana Historical Archives.

"Perhaps we could have stopped it": Letter from the parachutists to headquarters, September 26, 1944, in the Hagana Historical Archives.

Details of the raid on the safe house appear in *Mivtza Amsterdam* and in *Haviva Reick*.

Details of the sexual innuendo to which Haviva was subjected during training are from *Haviva Reick*.

The description of the reversal in Hungary in mid-October 1944 is drawn from Horthy's *Memoirs*.

"We're facing a situation in which we're forced to fight with our last strength": This letter from Egon Roth seems to be from July 1944. A Hebrew translation in the Hagana Historical Archives is stamped September 10, 1944.

Haim's description of the fall of the rebel enclave and the escape to the hills is from *Mivtza Amsterdam*.

NOTES ON SOURCES

"Our fate is bitter—and you have sent us new life.": This letter from Egon seems to have been attached to a dispatch from the parachutists sent on October 3, 1944. From the Hagana Historical Archives.

the first freedom fighters against the Nazis under Israeli command: From an interview with Haim, along with Joel Palgi, on the Israeli Public Broadcasting Authority youth TV program *Face to Face*, undated but probably from the early 1970s (https://www.youtube.com/watch?v=DeKm0tYpmBc).

The sketch of the site near Pohronský Bukovec, based on one made by Haim, is in the Hagana Historical Archives.

The authors of the accounts of the German attack in the forest, all in the Hagana Historical Archives, are as follows: Dr. Tyroler, from his report cited above; Hansi Weiss, a leader of the youth movement Hashomer Hatzair, who was in Haim's tent when the attack began, in testimony dated April 14, 1946; Aviva Markovitch, who survived the attack and later made it to Israel, in testimony dated March 6, 1946; an unidentified survivor of the attack in undated testimony; and Haim as quoted in a report from Mossad official Zvi Yehieli, who interviewed him in Cairo in May 1945 (letter dated May 7, 1945). Additional details are from *Mivtza Amsterdam* and from Haim's essay "A Camp of Jewish Fighters" in *Magen Baseter* (Secret Defender). In the essay, Haim writes that the soldiers were Ukrainians from the so-called Vlasov army, commanded by German sergeants and aided by a Slovak guide. According to Hansi Weiss, there were six fatalities in the attack, including Egon Roth.

The final letter from Zvi Ben-Yaakov was published in 1948 in *Magen Baseter* (Secret Defender). The letter is undated, but a footnote reads: "Written at the end of December 1944 and delivered to the Land at the end of the war."

The final letter from Rafi Reisz, dated November 19, 1944, was printed in the same volume. A footnote reads: "The letter was delivered to

NOTES ON SOURCES

the Land with the help of a member of the Slovak underground, a Christian, who was imprisoned with [Rafi], and who now holds an important role in the Czechoslovak government."

The report of a last letter from Haviva is from the testimony from Hansi Weiss, April 14, 1946, in the Hagana Historical Archives: "[A] report arrived from near Banská Bystrica according to which there is a female prison guard who has a letter from Haviva that was given to the guard before she was executed. A man was sent to check the veracity of the rumor. Hansi doesn't know the result."

7. THE MISSING

"Oh God! I will lose my mind from these reports!": Parachutist Dov Berger, writing to Hagana commanders from Bucharest on March 28, 1945. In the Hagana Historical Archives.

"According to a broadcast from a station that seems to be American": A report from December 22, 1944, signed by a Hagana official using the code name Haim (not Haim Hermesh the parachutist) who has just returned from Cairo with information from MI9 headquarters. In the Hagana Historical Archives.

"The rumor says he was wounded and died": Letter from unknown agent in Bucharest to Tel Aviv, February 27, 1945. In the Hagana Historical Archives.

"They were undoubtedly caught with partisans.": From the December 22, 1944, report from the official code-named Haim. In the Hagana Historical Archives.

A subsequent report arriving via Switzerland: Letter from Teddy Kollek to Wing Cmdr. Dennis of MI9, January 21, 1945. In the Hagana Historical Archives.

NOTES ON SOURCES

But the source acknowledges: Ofer and Ofer, *Haviva Reick*. The other woman is Aviva Markovich, who survived the attack and whose testimony is in the Hagana Historical Archives.

"A-Force mission dropped Pratomagno two months ago landed on Todt fortifications.": Message from Wing Cmdr. Dennis of MI9 to Hagana officials in Tel Aviv, October 18, 1944. In the Hagana Historical Archives.

The British War Office, citing information from the Red Cross: Internal Hagana communication, November 26, 1944, in the Hagana Historical Archives.

"I was happy to learn that Enzo is in touch with you": Letter from Capt. M. Nahimson to Capt. Rappoport, January 4, 1945, in the Hagana Historical Archives.

"information received leads us to think that Sereni was captured and shot": Message from Wing Cmdr. Dennis of MI9 to Tel Aviv, October 18, 1944. In the Hagana Historical Archives.

"Needless to say I wish to associate myself with W/Cdr Dennis' regret that so gallant a man has lost his life": Letter from Tony Simonds to Reuven Shiloah of the Hagana, October 22, 1944. In the Hagana Historical Archives.

The fourth-hand radio report regarding the fate of Sereni is noted in the Hagana Historical Archives, dated March 20, 1945. The member of Enzo's kibbutz who is the source is named as Uri Rosenblatt.

"In the Bonfires of War": Hannah Senesh, 1940. Original in the Hannah Senesh Collection at the National Library. Translation mine.

Lotem Faran's speech to troops in the fall of 2023 can be found here: https://www.facebook.com/watch/?v=3631522370502427.

The scene in the woods in which Hannah presses her poem into Dafni's hand was described on numerous occasions by Dafni over many years, including his interview in the documentary *Blessed Is the Match* and in video testimony from 1990 kept at Yad Vashem in Jerusalem. In his

NOTES ON SOURCES

early essay "The Last Border," Dafni mentions receiving the poem from Hannah but doesn't say when.

"Happy is the match that flared and lit the flames.": Hannah Senesh, 1944, translation mine. The original note is kept at the Ghetto Fighters' House Museum in northern Israel.

The Hannah Senesh skit from the satire show *Hayehudim Ba'im* (The Jews Are Coming), written by Yuval Friedman, was broadcast on Israeli public television, https://www.youtube.com/watch?v=AzPgQXiJD1w.

The podcast with the testimony from Zivia Lubetkin at the Eichmann trial is *Lech Tizkor* (Go Remember), from the Israeli public broadcaster Kan 11, May 6, 2024.

The conversation around the bonfire with Dafni, Hannah, and the Jewish partisan is recounted in Dafni's essay "The Last Border," in *Diaries*.

On June 20, two weeks after Hannah disappears: Internal Hagana report, dated June 20, 1944, in the Hagana Historical Archives. Dafni reported the same to headquarters on July 15.

The description of the Margit Körút military prison is dated December 24, 1944, in the Hagana Historical Archives. The description of the gendarmerie, from the same source, is dated December 1, 1944.

"We very much regret to inform you": Letter from Simonds to Reuven Zaslani of the Hagana, October 22, 1944, in the Hagana archive. The Anglicized spelling of her family name appears here in keeping with the usage throughout the text; in the original letter the name is spelled, accurately, "Szenes."

He copies the poem solemnly into his journal: Friling, *Arrows in the Dark*.

8. PRISON

The description of the scene in the Senesh house in Budapest on June 17, 1944, appears in Katherine's essay "Meeting in Budapest" in *Diaries*.

NOTES ON SOURCES

The description of how Hannah was captured, and of what happened in the subsequent days, is drawn from Tissandier's testimony in the Hagana Historical Archives. Joel Palgi's memoir also mentions that one of Hannah's front teeth was knocked or pulled out.

Ha-tzankhanit she-lo shava (The Parachutist Who Never Came Back) by Oded Betzer was published by Y. Sreberk Publishers in Tel Aviv in 1969.

"*Earlier, there was quite an event*": Hannah's diary, National Library, July 14, 1938.

"*My Lord—may these things never end*": Hannah Senesh, "A Walk to Caesarea," November 1942. Original in the Hannah Senesh Collection at the National Library. Translation mine.

a Ukrainian military choir: "Ukrainian army choir sings 'Eli Eli' on International Holocaust Memorial Day," *The Jerusalem Post*, January 28, 2023.

"*One, two, three . . . eight is the length.*": Hannah Senesh, 1944. Original in the Hannah Senesh Collection at the National Library. Translated from the Hungarian on my behalf by Agnes Kende.

Stefan Zweig's suicide note, from February 22, 1942, is preserved at Israel's National Library.

The Nazi documents, in German, are from the research volume *The Destruction of Hungarian Jewry: A Documentary Account* by Randolph L. Braham (Pro Arte for the World Federation of Hungarian Jews, 1963). They were translated for me by Esther Rachow.

The quotes from Joel's memoir are from the Hebrew edition, translation mine.

Katherine's description of her own arrest, imprisonment, and attempted suicide come from her essay in *Diaries*.

For opposing takes on the Kasztner Affair, see the two books mentioned here, by Porter and Bogdanor, as well as the engaging polemic *Perfidy* by Ben Hecht (Messner, 1961).

NOTES ON SOURCES

Details of Palgi's testimony at the trial in Jerusalem and his tortured association with Kasztner (who had been his counselor in a youth movement in Hungary before the war) can be found in the 2003 introduction to the English edition of Palgi's memoir by David Engel, a Holocaust scholar at New York University, and in the review of the same book in *Haaretz* by Judith Tydor Baumel-Schwartz of Bar-Ilan University on June 13, 2003.

In Gestapo custody Joel remembers a scene from earlier that year: From Palgi's memoir.

The aftermath of Katherine's failed suicide attempt and the subsequent days and weeks in the prison: From Katherine's essay in *Diaries*.

The scene inside the prison during and after the Arrow Cross coup are described by Palgi in his memoir.

The grandfather of a friend of mine: The murdered man was Ephraim Erwin Steiner, a former Austro-Hungarian army officer and veteran of the First World War whose parents named him for Emperor Franz Joseph, like many Austro-Hungarian Jews named Ephraim or Ephraim-Joseph in the emperor's honor. His grandson is Israeli history professor Ephraim Shoham-Steiner of Ben-Gurion University.

issued after the collapse of communist Hungary: Documents from the Hungarian military court, July–August 1993, communicated to the Israeli government and preserved in the Hagana Historical Archives.

The description of the 1944 trial and of the days around Hannah's execution: From Palgi's memoir and from Katherine's account in *Diaries*.

"Dear Mother, I don't know what to say.": Hannah's final note is kept in the National Library in Jerusalem.

9. HAIM

Haim's account of the weeks in the Slovak woods after the attack at the camp, and of the subsequent months with the partisans, are from *Mivtza Amsterdam*.

NOTES ON SOURCES

Haim's meeting with Zvi Yehieli in Cairo is described in Zvi's letter of May 7, 1945, in the Hagana Historical Archives. According to Yehieli, he spent a week with Haim, hearing about his "perilous wanderings."

I interviewed Shaul Hermesh and Rafi Hermesh, Haim's sons, in July 2023.

The forensic report from Slovakia with details on Haviva (body No. 209) is included with a letter from November 16, 1945, from Maj. W. H. Stewart to Teddy Kollek of the Jewish Agency for Israel, in the Hagana Historical Archives. She was declared "killed in action" on September 1, 1945. Body No. 176 in the same mass grave at Kremnička was that of Rafi Reisz.

10. AFTERLIFE

Details of Ada Sereni's mission to Italy are from the academic article by Lilach Rosenberg-Friedman, "Unforgettable Heroine? The Place and Status of Ada Sereni in the Collective Memory," in *Cathedra* 137 (Fall 2010): 147–78. Additional details are from Ada's book *Sfinot lelo degel* (Ships with No Flag), 1975, first published in Italian in 1973 as *I clandestini del mare*.

Ada's first stop is the headquarters of MI9 in Cairo: A note of introduction to Simonds is in the Hagana Historical Archives, dated June 7, 1945.

"I much regret that there is still no information on Dr. SERENI's location": Letter from Billie Neville of MI9 to Teddy Kolleck, June 23, 1945. In the Central Zionist Archives.

"There was no point in hiding anything from her.": Internal communication, July 10, 1945, Central Zionist Archives.

"in the special bloc for Englishmen": Letter from Ada to Mossad superiors, September 7, 1945, in the Central Zionist Archives.

"Enzo alive exhausted in hospital Russian zone Ada on way to him.": Telegram dated October 12, 1945, from Teddy Kollek to Moshe Shertok (Sharett), in the Central Zionist Archives. Hagar Sereni's

NOTES ON SOURCES

memory of her response to hearing this news is in the essay by Lilach Rosenberg-Friedman.

I visited the Dachau memorial and archive in April 2024 and am grateful to Miriam Weber and the rest of the archive staff for their assistance.

In Ada's memoir, she recounts that she learned the fact and date of Enzo's death when an officer of the Jewish Brigade brought her a copy of the Dachau prisoner card to Milan. She writes: "My private mission was over."

The Palmach fighter whom I interviewed about the beaching of the ship *Hannah Senesh* was Isaac Shoshan, one of the heroes of my book *Spies of No Country* (2019).

"A 40-year-old woman is progressing toward the end and can't waste years.": Letter from Ada in Milan to her children at Givat Brenner, December 31, 1945. Quoted in the essay by Lilach Rosenberg-Friedman.

What her father did, she says, was selfish: From Enzo's grandson, historian Alon Confino, in the Hebrew essay "My grandfather Enzo Sereni," *Hazman Hazeh*, August 2014.

"I know that I won't be a simple worker. I can't be and don't want to be," becomes merely, "I think I won't be a simple worker.": Dayan, "Between Hannah and St. Joan."

"Of course, Aniko, of course!" answers Katherine. "Could you have done otherwise?": This line, from the play *Hannah Senesh* by Aharon Megged, is quoted in Dayan's thesis.

a box was buried containing Hannah's possessions: This assertion appears in the final essay in *Diaries*, titled "With Her Inheritance," by the editor and historian Moshe Breslawski (1903–1961).

ACKNOWLEDGMENTS

I'd like to thank my friend and colleague Israel Rosner, who first suggested I look into the story of the parachutists. Yehuda Wegman—former military officer, historian, and a curator at the museum dedicated to Hannah Senesh at Kibbutz Sdot Yam—gave me valuable advice early on. Historian and guide Moshe Harmatz, a font of knowledge about this Israeli story and many others, lent me a few rare books and took me on a trip to Hungary and Slovakia that allowed me to bring parts of this story to life.

I'm grateful to my first readers and best critics, my parents, Imogene and Raphael Friedman; to my agent Deborah Harris, and to George Eltman; and to my editors, Doug Pepper in Toronto and Cindy Spiegel in New York. Translators Esther Rachow (German), Agnes Kende (Hungarian), and Rocco Blume (Italian) illuminated key details. Thanks to friends and colleagues who read the manuscript as it evolved: Benjamin Balint, Nicole Krauss, Jonathan Safran Foer, and Ksenia Tserkovskaya. Thanks to Simon Sebag Montefiore for his generous encouragement. And thanks to my wife, Naama, and to Aviv, Michael, Tamar, and Asaf, for spending years with yet more strange and invisible characters in the house.

Two young men whom I knew, both from Jerusalem, both lovers of people and books, were consumed by war as I worked on this story: Hersh Goldberg-Polin and Yuval Shoham. This book is dedicated to their memory.

PHOTO CREDITS

Photograph of Hannah Senesh: Courtesy of the Szenes Family Archive, with thanks to Ori and Mirit Eisen, the National Library of Israel collections.

Photograph of Lt. Col. Anthony Simonds OBE: Courtesy of his daughter, Rosey Woollcombe, and the Simonds family website (www.simondsfamily.me.uk).

Photograph of Enzo Sereni: From the Bitmuna collection. Photographer: Hanan Bahir.

Photograph of Haviva Reick: Courtesy of the Kibbutz Maanit archive.

Map of the site of the camp near Bukovec, Slovakia: Courtesy of the Hagana Historical Archives, Tel Aviv.

Photograph of Haim Hermesh: Courtesy of the Hermesh family.

ABOUT THE AUTHOR

Matti Friedman was born in Toronto and lives in Jerusalem. He is the author of four previous works of nonfiction: *Who by Fire: Leonard Cohen in the Sinai* (2022); *Spies of No Country: Secret Lives at the Birth of Israel* (2019); *Pumpkinflowers: A Soldier's Story of a Forgotten War* (2016); and *The Aleppo Codex* (2012). His books have won numerous prizes and have been translated into more than a dozen languages. A columnist for *The Free Press*, his journalistic work has appeared in *The Atlantic*, *The New York Times*, *Smithsonian*, and elsewhere.